SECRET SOCIETIES

AND THE

HERMETIC CODE

The Rosicrucian, Masonic, and Esoteric Transmission in the Arts

ERNESTO FRERS

TRANSLATED BY ARIEL GODWIN

Destiny Books
Rochester, Vermont

Destiny Books
One Park Street
Rochester, Vermont 05767
www.DestinyBooks.com

Destiny Books is a division of Inner Traditions International

Originally published in Spanish under the title *El museo secreto* by Ediciones Robinbook, Barcelona
First U.S. edition published in 2008 by Destiny Books

Library of Congress Cataloging-in-Publication Data
Frers, Ernesto.
  [Museo secreto. English]
  Secret societies and the hermetic code : the Rosicrucian, Masonic, and esoteric transmission in the arts / Ernesto Frers ; translated by Ariel Godwin.
     p. cm.
  Includes bibliographical references and index.
  ISBN: 978-1-59477-208-5 (pbk.)
  1. Hermetism in art. 2. Hermetism in music. I. Title.
  N8217.H57F7413 2008
  700'.47—dc22

                                                      2007053066

Printed and bound in Canada by Transcontinental Printing

10 9 8 7 6 5 4 3 2 1

Text design and layout by Priscilla Baker
This book was typeset in Garamond, with Trajan and Gill Sans used as display typefaces.

CONTENTS

INTRODUCTION

Every work of art is a message transmitted by the author to his contemporaries and, if he is lucky, to posterity. This message is usually visible and obvious, directed toward the emotions, sentiments, feelings, intellect, and interests of the hypothetical spectator. A few exceptional artists have produced great works of art that have gained unanimous and enduring acceptance during the course of time. Many of these artists did not limit themselves to painting a picture, creating a sculpture, designing a building, or writing a musical score but also included in their works certain secret symbols and messages directed at the initiated.

In ancient civilizations, art was closely linked to pagan cults, which in turn were linked to Hermeticism and magic. The rulers and high priests who commissioned the artworks wanted them to reflect the theogony and occult knowledge that gave them their power. As a result, these monuments, friezes, and statues held meanings that were not understandable to these leaders' everyday subjects.

Without a doubt, the culminating point of art containing esoteric messages was in the Middle Ages and the Renaissance. The Church's severe censure of everything that was not connected to it forced artists to use religious works to conceal mystical and Hermetic references that had little or nothing to do with the images or scenes depicted. The underground presence of pagan cults and the thaumaturgy of the

Celtic Druids frequently emerged from behind sacred art. In addition, the Byzantine schism brought with it the use of inverted perspective and a number of occult rules that the popes of the orthodox Church and their faithful considered sacred. During the early Middle Ages, the Order of the Temple was influential in the rise of the Gothic style, leading to the construction of splendid cathedrals built with secret techniques that used Hermetic proportions to transmit their mysterious message.

The burgeoning of the Renaissance—especially in Italy—brought about not only a revival of classical art but also a strong intellectual movement in literary circles and academies, involving figures such as Nicholas of Cusa, Marsilio Ficino, and Pico della Mirandola, who studied and revolutionized Pythagorean and Platonic Hermeticism, the kabbalah, and other mysteries linked to Hermes Trismegistus. Artists frequented these circles, often as initiates or disciples, and it was not a rarity for them to integrate into their works symbols and messages that related to their esoteric creed.

Works that contained enigmas and occult meanings were also produced before and after this era of special connectedness of Hermeticism and art. From ancient Egyptian monuments to Greek sculptures, from Tenebrist painting to dreamlike Surrealism, over the course of its history, art has held hidden symbols that connect its cryptic messages to the mysteries of the great esoteric tradition.

THE SECRET MUSEUM

This book intends to bring together a selection of those great works that allow for a double or triple reading, forming a kind of secret museum that the reader can visit virtually, with the aid of the illustrations that accompany the text. I have attempted to choose the most representative works within each era and discipline, including some pieces whose esotericism is particularly unusual or little known. The result is necessarily incomplete, but in my belief, this text presents substantial examples of the connection between artistic genius and an interest in the mystical dimension of the universe.

To this imaginary secret museum there is added a small concert hall in which we review a few examples from a vast number of musical compositions influenced by Hermeticism. In this case, the sections are arranged not by work but by era and author—a more appropriate approach for understanding such musical development.

Those who approach this book without prejudice will be able to confirm the existence of these secret messages at the turning of each page. I hope you will enjoy reading this text in much the same way as did the artists who created these masterpieces: with a mind and spirit open to the unknown.

PAINTING

Drawing and painting are primordial abilities in human culture and have always been connected to magical and religious symbolism. Their first known manifestations were in so-called rock art, which emerged with the European *Homo sapiens* during the Upper Paleolithic period, about forty thousand years ago.

In ancient and classical Western civilizations, the locations for paintings were the walls, friezes, columns, and facades of temples and other monuments. Painting as an entirely independent work—what we now call pictures—emerged in Europe in the form of Christian iconography produced on panels and altarpieces. Later, the canvas stretched over a frame and mounted on an easel became more widespread.

In the chronological order in which works are presented here, inevitably there is a greater weight placed upon those pieces created between the fifteenth and seventeenth centuries. This is not only because this era produced such a great number of brilliant artists and masterpieces in the unfolding of the Renaissance but also because it produced a great number of paintings containing esoteric symbols and Hermetic messages—indeed, more than ever before. In its revisionist examination of the past, Renaissance culture produced a new kind of profane philosophy, setting aside Christian theology and recovering the Hermetic sources of antiquity and their arcane mysteries. Yet the principal patrons of the arts continued to be the popes, the prelates, and the aristocrats connected to the Church, which prohibited as heresy all occultist readings and practices and even punished these with death. In order to avoid being discovered, artists such as Botticelli, Hieronymus Bosch, and Leonardo da Vinci carefully concealed within their works secret allusions to their esoteric convictions and wisdom. This was also the case for patrons who were adept in the occult sciences, such as Duke Cosimo de Medici in Florence, who expected his artists to include in their works symbols and allusions referring to the mystical creed they—and he—professed.

The rationalistic rise of the Enlightenment and modernity caused an apparent decline in Hermetic knowledge, especially in connection to a pictorial art that was becoming individualistic and mundane. Despite this decline, some examples of nineteenth- and twentieth-century masterpieces with esoteric messages are included here.

EASTERN CHRISTIAN ART:
BYZANTINE, RUSSIAN, GREEK, AND SLAVIC

The religious art of Byzantium (such as icons created beginning in the sixth century) rejected the realism of Western painting and stuck with hieratic images and inverted perspective, following a few strict, formal rules of sacred and metaphysical character. (See plate 1.)

Mystic Windows on a Higher Plane

Byzantine religious icons are not works of art in our Western way of understanding but instead are coded messages communicating to the observer the Divine on a mystical and otherworldly plane. The artists who painted them did not consider these works simply religious images but instead viewed them as sacred mediating objects that put the icons in contact with the energies of the celestial being they represented. This was also the case for the priests and worshippers who venerated them in churches or carried on journeys small icons covered by a pair of wooden doors that could be opened at the time of prayer. This manner of veneration still continues today between Eastern and Orthodox Christians.

Painting Other Realities

The light and colors of icons do not attempt to represent reality; they do not imitate earthly colors and light but instead represent certain keys for facilitating mystic trances in believers. Gilded illumination does not come from the sun or from another light source, nor does it produce shadows. Instead, it comes from another dimension that is comprehensible only to priests and initiated believers.

Iconography's symbolic use follows strict Hermetic formulas whose symbols have developed over the course of centuries. Among the most obvious is the use of gilded frames and backgrounds that are covered entirely in gold leaf. These symbolize and define the supernatural significance placed upon the scenes or figures illustrated. The symbols in the icons appear in limited, preestablished variations and preserve

Christ Pantocrator.
Despite their inaccuracies,
icons preserve magnificent
expressiveness and
plenitude.

a strictly codified hieratic perspective based on predetermined methods of interpretation. Their appearance does not aspire to a naturalistic reproduction of Christ, the Virgin, the saints, or the gospel scenes. On the contrary, heads appear to be spread out, simultaneously showing the forehead and the temples or sometimes the upper part of the skull, while bodies often exhibit a disproportion between the trunk and limbs or chest and shoulders or, if they are kneeling, exaggerated hunched backs. The faces tend toward a uniform abstraction (which might be called "icon face"), with a long and straight nose that is sometimes outlined, a very small and well-defined mouth, and large eyes staring into emptiness as if they are gazing at an interior universe. The hands, schematic and elongated, often form mysterious signs with the fingers.

These "errors" in depiction are not due to the clumsiness or inexperience of new artists but to a premeditated and devised deconstruction of forms according to strict codes. The icons reflect another reality based on its own system of perception and representation. A painter of icons likely did not consider himself an artist or a creator in accordance with the Western view of art because his task was simply to produce another copy of a prototype by following inflexible rules and techniques established by his predecessors. Yet the pride he took in his work was no less than, for example, that of a Renaissance master. His work was a mystic talisman, a window into a mysterious, sacred dimension, and through this he himself was a demiurge, an interpreter capable of providing his fellow believers with a path to revelation.

Sacred Perspective

One characteristic of Byzantine icons is that they present gross errors and contradictions in terms of the linear perspective imposed on all Western art since the Renaissance. In the early twentieth century, the Russian theorist Pavel Florensky attacked this view of the treatment of space in works of art, describing linear perspective as a mere conventional form that did not represent reality.

In his book *La perspectiva invertida* (The Inverted Perspective), Florensky presents a fervent and erudite defense of iconographic errors, pointing out that linear perspective is not real and does not coincide with the human visual experience. "People do not see in perspective," he claims, "and it took half a millennium of education for us to observe and depict the world in this artificial manner." In his analysis of the system rediscovered in the fifteenth century by Giotto, he recalls that perspective originated from a deception of the eye invented by Aeschylus and Anaxagoras in classical Greece in order to make the scenery for tragedies more realistic. It was a theatrical, scenographic deception that had very little to do with the optical perception of a human being looking at the world.

Inverted perspective, on the other hand, does not attempt to represent what the human eye sees but precisely what it does not see. Figures grow in size and importance as they get farther away, because they come from a more distant world. Planes intersect; buildings show their facade and sides at the same time or their roofs are open because they belong to another dimension. The entire picture reflects not the view of the carnal eye but that of the divine eye indicated in some icons by distinct vanishing points.

The mystical perspective of icons stands in opposition to the symbolic perspective of the Renaissance. Such is faith in its sacred character: Even when symbolic perspective prevailed over all Europe in the sixteenth century, the painters of icons and the orthodox prelates who employed these artists continued applying mystical perspective unperturbedly through the subsequent centuries, convinced without a doubt that the purpose of art is not to duplicate reality but to capture its essence and its most profound meaning.

The Rebellion of the Iconoclasts

Founded in the late fourth century, the Eastern Roman Empire began to develop artistic forms that were truly Byzantine (named after the Empire's capital, Byzantium, now Istanbul), expressed in architecture, paintings, and mosaics. These pictorial works were designated by the Greek word *eikón,* meaning "image," which has passed down to us as *icon.* In the first golden age of Byzantine art, during the reign of Justinian in the sixth century, the term was reserved for painted religious tablets at the temple that bore details in gold leaf and gilded or silver-plated frames.

The presence of icons in Byzantine churches was questioned by so-called *iconoclasts,* who were opposed to the worship of images. This movement emerged in the late seventh century in the southern regions of the Byzantine Empire, which were receiving strong pressure from the Muslims. Islam's rejection of depictions of religious figures and, along with this rejection, the legacy of Aristotelianism coming from Greece had a hand in the expansion of a powerful and combative movement against the veneration of icons in Orthodox temples. Opposed to the iconoclasts were the *iconodules,* defenders of the symbolic and educational value of icons. For them, the image of Christ was the Word itself made flesh, and not depicting it meant negating this divine incarnation.

After a number of serious conflicts, the iconoclasts finally prevailed, and in 730 the Byzantine emperor Leo III ordered the destruction and prohibition of all images representing divine persons and saints. This edict resulted in the loss of countless invaluable icons from the preceding centuries, although many were saved. Clerics hid them in the temples and the faithful kept them concealed, even when the secret possession or veneration of these works was classed as idolatry and was punishable by mutilation.

Despite the extreme severity of these measures, the common people refused to give up the images that functioned as reference points and confirmation for their faith. Iconoclasm prevailed amid a climate of unrest and popular resistance, which was used to advantage by theologians and intellectual iconodules such as St. John of Damascus, the last of the Eastern Fathers. His speeches and writings influenced Pope Adrian I, who, in 787, summoned the Second Council of Nicaea (the Seventh Ecumenical Council). The council's conclusions recommended reestablishing the worship of images—but the iconoclasts would not renounce their position, and the dispute continued for the next five decades until another council was convened in Constantinople under the new Byzantine emperor Michael III. Here, the definitive rejection of iconoclasm was consecrated, and the next year, with solemn festivities, the whole Eastern Empire celebrated the return of the icons to churches and the homes of the faithful.

The Symbolism of the Iconostasis

The triumph of the iconodules coincided with an era of cultural elevation encouraged by Platonic esotericism and Greek Hermeticism. The priests and theologians of the Eastern Church adopted ideas of secret and transcendental symbolism while at the same time establishing canonical norms for the production and placement of icons. Thus, very rigid rules were established for twelve depictions of the Virgin Mary, and the image of Christ Pantocrator (God, Lord of the Universe) was painted with a bearded face and a stern frown, with one hand raised to form the mystic sign of his power (the index and middle fingers pointing up and the other fingers folded over the palm).

In 1054, the East-West Schism divided Christianity into two autonomous churches, the Catholic and the Orthodox. After this time, the Orthodox Church enjoyed freedom from Rome both to establish its liturgies and to devise a symbolic manner of placing icons in its temples. Icon placement ascends, and the specific positioning of the images signifies a spiritual transition into the divine realm. Illustrations from the gospel are placed in the lower part of the temple and above them appears a procession of bishops with the Paschal Lamb or the infant Jesus on a paten. In the apse there is one of the twelve representations of the Virgin, and above, the all-powerful Pantocrator presides over everything from the top of the dome.

In the following centuries, peculiar novelties were introduced such as the representation of the Mandylion, the sacred cloth with the true face of Christ imprinted on it (see color plate 1). The Orthodox consider this controversial relic as proof and testimony of the sanctity of icons because they believe the image contains the energies of the divine person it represents. The depiction of the Last Supper also saw more emphasis due to the influence of gnosticism and the doctrinal assumption of the Hermetic principle of "as above, so below"; the liturgy celebrated on earth is the imitation of that which is celebrated by Christ in heaven.

The Orthodox religion expanded throughout Greece, Russia, Bulgaria, Romania, and the Balkans, where it continues to prevail today and where prized icons with their esoteric code and inverted perspective are still worshipped. Western art, in contrast, continued for centuries its allegiance to linear perspective and realistic anatomy—until Picasso and his cubist contemporaries shattered these rules in the manner of the best Byzantine demiurge painters.

SANDRO BOTTICELLI
PRIMAVERA
(1477)

The great fifteenth-century artist linked to Renaissance paganism and occultism included various initiatory symbols in *Primavera* (Uffizi Gallery, Florence). The painting's characters, taken from classical mythology, form a scene filled with Hermetic allusions. (See color plates 2–3.)

Allegory of an Initiatory Mystery
It should be noted that the original title Botticelli gave this painting was *Allegory of Springtime* because the scene does not depict a climatic season but a series of symbolic elements expressing something apart from their apparent meaning. The canvas, rendered in oil and tempera, is a single great panel of about 80 × 124 inches, a common size for religious paintings in the Renaissance but unusual for secular works. This indicates the importance Botticelli placed upon this painting, whose dimensions suggest the complexity and transcendence hidden behind its supposedly decorative theme.

Corresponding to the time of year in which nature renews herself by showing all her splendor, *Primavera* depicts a bucolic scene filled with grace and color. In front of a background of a forest of fruit trees there are depicted eight figures, two by themselves and six grouped in two trios.

Mythological Characters
Botticelli drew all his characters from classical mythology, giving them an allegorical appearance. The scene can be read from right to left, like Hebrew writing or like Leonardo da Vinci's notes and some Hermetic texts. Starting on the right, we see Zephyr, the god of the winds, flying in and grabbing a young woman from behind, perhaps driving her forward with his divine breath. The maiden in question, representing the nymph Chloris, heads the group of six female figures that continues with

Flora (springtime), the only one who is definitely advancing toward the viewer. Further on, occupying the center of the scene, we see Venus, the goddess of love, somewhat isolated and standing still. At the top center, flying above Venus and very near the upper border of the painting, there is Cupid in his usual form as a small angel, drawing back his bow with his eyes blindfolded. Further to the left, the Three Graces are dancing with their hands entwined. The picture ends with the distracted youth at the far left, who represents Mercury, the messenger of the Roman gods and himself the god of commerce and eloquence.

The Esoteric Symbols

Sandro Botticelli was not simply a painter of the religious and secular themes typical of the Renaissance; as we will see later, he was a man initiated into the mysterious paganism that pervaded the intellectual and artistic circles of this era. Iconologists who explore the secret messages and symbols in works of art always show a particular interest in deciphering the occult codes underlying the mythological bucolicism of *Primavera*.

According to the most widely accepted esoteric interpretation, the entire painting expresses a Hermetic description of the spiritual being's voyage into the material reality of the manifest world. Each of the different characters represents an element in this journey, making his or her inclusion consistent in the scene depicted. Let us see what these elements are and what they tell us as we read them in the proper direction, from right to left.

Zephyr's greenish blue color is not a caprice on the artist's part. This strange and unique chromatic shade distinguishes him clearly from the other figures who make up the scene. In classical mythology, Zephyr was the young god of springtime, and a soft breeze scattered the flowers gathered in his cloak. In Botticelli's painting, this flowery function corresponds to Flora, whose serene beauty contrasts with the god's sullen face and livid complexion. We should now understand that Zephyr is not actually a god and does not form part of any imaginary

The god Zephyr uses his divine breath to push the nymph Chloris into the scene.

Olympus, much less the real or manifest world. As the god he appears to be, he represents the force of wind, but a wind of the subterranean world that rises up from a different dimension, pushing forward the nymph Chloris simply to introduce her into the scene.

Who, then, is Chloris? Her name suggests clarity, light, and the color white, symbolizing innocent purity. She is the pure and luminous soul that must confront the karmic process; she is shoved forward by the secret energy of life in its journey toward spiritual perfection. In the painting, the nymph turns her face toward her captor with an expression that suggests a certain fear or resistance before this force that pushes her and obliges her to transform herself. The painter has captured her in the moment of being transformed into Flora, the brilliant beauty of springtime as symbolized by her flowery costume and her triumphal advance toward the exterior of the painting (possibly the real world).

Botticelli conveyed this transfiguration in a detail of the two figures: For each one, the right foot is in exactly the same position at an equal distance from the bottom edge of the painting. While Chloris is standing on her right foot in order to lift her left one, Flora's left foot is forward, placed on the ground, thus completing the movement begun by Chloris. Together, the two represent the same initiatory path.

Some who have interpreted the secret language of *Primavera* have claimed that these three figures on the right side of the canvas comprise their own theme in addition to their role in the secret message of the

Flora, with her flowery garments, symbolizes springtime.

work in its entirety. Zephyr, who belongs to an Orphic dimension and cannot enter the manifest world, introduces Chloris into it; by changing into Flora, Chloris transmits the power of incarnating springtime. For this reason, Flora carries at her side the flowers that the mythological Zephyr carried in his cloak and assumes his function, scattering them in the earthly dimension. Moreover, because Chloris represents the spirit in its pure state, she begins her human transition as springtime, the season that symbolizes the young phase of life.

The Triadic Venus

It is uncommon to find a fully clothed Venus in mythologically themed art, especially when there are four nearly naked nymphs in the same work. Botticelli's Venus bears more resemblance to depictions of the

Botticelli's Venus bears more resemblance to depictions of the Virgin Mary than to those of the goddess of eroticism.

Virgin Mary than to those of the goddess of eroticism. In adopting this criterion for his central character, the artist was obviously giving her Hermetic significance. In keeping with his affiliation to Florentine Neoplatonism, Botticelli shows her completely dressed. It is known that Plato conceived the goddess as a cosmic duality: Venus Urania, celestial and naked, and Venus Pandemos, terrestrial and clothed. Further, because the scene involves a journey through initiatory experience into the manifest world, it must be Pandemos who presides. From this position, Venus's body, glance, and free hand are directed toward the Three Graces, a posture in which some authors see a triadic projection of the goddess. The three nymphs are dancing with their hands interlaced, forming a circle. The one on the left, Voluptas (voluptuousness), raises her left arm to clasp the right hand of Pulchritudo (beauty), forming a

The three nymphs, dancing with their hands interlaced, form a circle that symbolizes the wheel of life.

kind of protecting gesture over the head of Castitas (chastity). Voluptas advances forward, as if offering herself to Castitas, and Castitas steps backward in a receiving posture while Pulchritudo stretches upward in a turning gesture.

The interlaced hands of the three nymphs thus form the essential Orphic circle of *emanatio, raptio, et remeatio* (which can be translated as "give, accept, and give back"). This is both the cycle of initiation and the wheel of life. In this esoteric context, Castitas, symbol of purity, is looking toward Mercury as if she hopes he will turn toward her.

The Thrice-Great God

In fact, the god depicted by Botticelli is not the Roman Mercury but his Greek predecessor Hermes, called Trismegistus (three times great). The god of wisdom and writing, he is considered the generator of true occult knowledge, which through him gains the adjective Hermetic. Hermes Trismegistus is actually the Greek version of Thoth, the Egyptian god who ruled thaumaturgy and the secret power of the word and who (according to certain sources) was a priest who rose to divinity in ancient times. Hermes was believed to have written a series of mysterious books about this sacred knowledge, which were collected in the so-called *Corpus Hermeticum*. Worship of him as the protector of magic, alchemy, astrology, and the kabbalah was revived in the Middle Ages.

In the painting, Hermes holds in his right hand the caduceus (an olive branch with serpentlike garlands): the symbol of his power that sends the energy of life to a superior plane represented by golden fruit. There his energy will be received by Cupid, who passes it on to Zephyr, who in turn gives this renewed energy through Chloris-Flora. The occult meaning of *Primavera* is therefore the initiatory and vital cycle of *emanatio, raptio, et remeatio,* an essential principle for Renaissance Neoplatonists.

As for Cupid (in fact, the Greek Eros), who surveys the scene with blindfolded eyes, his Orphic significance establishes him as the primordial god of love. This is the divine love that creates the universe and instills life—but he is shown with a blindfold over his eyes because he also represents blind, innocent, ignorant love, possessing the *docta igno-rantia* that Nicholas of Cusa ascribed to the "learned ignorant."

An Initiated Artist

Born in 1444 as the youngest of the four sons of a Florentine tanner, Alessandro (Sandro) di Mariano Filipepi was called Botticelli (little bar-rel), a nickname given to the whole family due to the obesity of the oldest brother, Giovanni. At a very young age, Sandro worked as an apprentice in Pietro Pollaiolo's studio and also frequented Verrocchio's studio. The delicate lines of his sketches and his unique use of color awakened the interest of the Medici, who brought him under their protection.

The court of generous patron of the arts Lorenzo de Medici was

Sandro Botticelli included in his works occult symbols and messages that only initiates could read.

the center of the intense intellectual and artistic life of the Florentine Renaissance under the influence of the Platonic Academy founded by Cosimo de Medici. The young Sandro Botticelli had as his tutor Giorgio Antonio Vespucci, a neighbor of Botticelli's father and a relative of the famous Amerigo, who gave the New World its name. Vespucci belonged to the same circles as Marsilio Ficino and Angelo Poliziano, Neoplatonist academics who initiated Sandro into Orphic cosmogony and the secrets of the *Corpus Hermeticum.* They also introduced him to the reading of Homeric hymns as well as Ovid's *Fasti* and Horace's Odes, poetry inspired by the esotericism of Pythagoras and Plato.

Botticelli, like other artists of the epoch, became a fervent adept of Hermetic Mysteries and took advantage of his patrons' commissions, placing in his works occult symbols and messages that only initiates could read. *Primavera,* painted between 1477 and 1478, was commissioned by Pierfrancesco de Medici, a cousin of Lorenzo the Magnificent. A few years later, around 1485, the painter brought together some of the same characters in *Birth of Venus,* in which the goddess emerges naked from the waters upon a great seashell, blown by Zephyr (this time closely accompanied by Aura, another wind goddess) while Spring, or Flora, approaches Venus on the shore to cover her with her flowery cloak. The occult message is similar to that of *Primavera,* although this painting is ruled by Venus Urania of the celestial plane.

The Florentine artist also painted frescoes in the Sistine Chapel and illustrated a manuscript of the *Divine Comedy* by Dante Alighieri (another well-known adept of esotericism). In his later years, Botticelli fell under the influence of the fundamentalist monk Girolamo Savonarola and created only religious paintings that were greatly inferior in their execution to his earlier masterpieces.

Despite such changes of fortune, it is probable that Botticelli was more than just an initiate in the Orphic Mysteries and that he rose to higher planes in the community of mysterious scholars. In the controversial *Prieuré Documents* in the Bibliothèque Nationale in Paris, the painter of *Primavera* is listed as the grand master of the Priory of Sion

Botticelli's Birth of Venus *has an occult message similar to that of* Primavera.

from 1483 until his death in 1510. Even if such documents are considered apocryphal, their authors must have had some reason for placing this artist in such a high office. It is conjectured that the Priory may be one of the many facades used by the mysterious and wise followers of Thoth, and some scholars are certain that Botticelli was one of them.

PIERO DI COSIMO
THE DEATH OF PROCRIS
(ca. 1500)

This tragic mythological scene (now housed in the National Gallery, London) conceals behind its extreme chromatism and various secret symbols a great elegy to the Hermetic science practiced by the lunatic and unsociable artist. (See color plate 4.)

The Mysteries of Alchemy in a Chest

The Death of Procris, like many other works concerning the deaths of legendary or mythological characters, shows a half-naked body lying with its face wearing a placid expression and accompanied by one or more grieving relatives. In this case, Piero di Cosimo depicted the deceased nymph lying on her right side in a flowery meadow and occupying almost the whole length of the painting. On the left side of the painting, a handsome young faun kneels at her head. On the other side of the painting, opposite him, a large brownish dog with grieving loyalty watches over the dead woman. In the background—a sandy beach and an entirely blue landscape—we see two dogs, a black cat, and various birds flying, standing, or swimming in the grayish water.

Experts have pointed out the oddity of this work, beginning with its unusual format: an exaggerated rectangle. Piero di Cosimo did not hesitate to accept all types of commissions, from painting arches for carnival festivals to designing scenes for tapestries or decorating furniture. He probably painted this work for a wedding, as a frontispiece for a *cassone,* the large chest in which the wedding gifts and nuptial trousseau were kept. Long and low pieces of furniture such as these cassoni appear in various paintings from the era and are often depicted adorned with a frontal painting. The format of *The Death of Procris* (about 25.5 × 72 inches) corresponds to the measurements of some of these chests whose decorators used the technique of oil and tempera on board that was also employed by Piero di Cosimo.

A Florentine cassone *made in 1472 by Jacopo Sellaio.* The Death of Procris *was probably the frontispiece for a similar chest.*

Jealousy and Mistrust

The subject of the painting relates to a wedding, for it is inspired by the mythological story of a recently married couple: the hunter Cephalus and the nymph Procris, protégés of the goddess Diana. According to Ovid's poem narrating the fable (in the *Metamorphoses*), the youth decides to test his wife's fidelity and disguises himself in order to seduce her as someone else, but Procris guesses his true identity and flees disconsolately in search of Diana. Both Diana and Cephalus succeed in calming her, and the couple resume their conjugal life. Soon afterward, however, Procris begins to doubt her husband's faithfulness. One day, when Cephalus goes off hunting in the forest, she follows him silently. The young hunter mistakes her for his quarry amid the bushes and shoots her with an arrow, piercing her throat. Procris dies instantly, leaving Cephalus distraught.

Procris, the victim of jealousy, is mortally wounded by an arrow shot by Cephalus at what he thought was his quarry.

Although the story could be understood as an edifying warning for newlyweds, it does not seem very appropriate as a decoration for the occasion of a wedding. It is not known whether the work's commissioner also indicated its design or whether this was chosen by the devious imagination of the artist, whose unbalanced and eccentric talent was known all over Florence.

An Elegy to Alchemy

In his strange illustration of the fable of Cephalus and Procris, the artist included a series of symbols and codes relating to the mysteries of alchemy. The faun represents a savage and innocent being who existed before Original Sin. Here he places his hand on the left shoulder of the dead nymph, behind whom there is a slender tree rising in front of the bluish background. Alchemists believed that the original, or primal, substance emerged from the cadaver of a member of the primordial couple (Adam or Eve) in the form of the philosophical or Hermetic tree, which represented resurrection and immortality, similarly to the kabbalists' Tree of Life.

Alchemy probably also drew from the kabbalah the enigmatic principle that "the place of God is the world, but the world is not the place of God." Piero di Cosimo used for the background of this work a flat, otherworldly landscape without the customary vanishing points of Renaissance perspective—a landscape in which the sky, water, hills, and buildings are all suffused with the same cold and unreal blue. It is a world that is not the place of God and could perhaps be our world seen as a bleak underworld. Nature reappears in the foreground, where the forms and colors are real and give verisimilitude to the characters.

The painter removed from the scene Cephalus, Procris's involuntary murderer, replacing him with the Apollonian faun, who does not appear in the version of the legend told by Ovid in the *Metamorphoses*. His inclusion in the painting may be due to Piero di Cosimo's taste for depicting fantastical beings—but it should also be noted that the faun is formally known as Faunus Lupercus (he who protects from the wolf). In the feasts of Lupercalia, honor was paid to adolescent Roman youths who, according to custom, had lived for some time as savages in the forest. In certain alchemical books, the faun was one of the symbols of the pure, original substance necessary for undertaking the Great Work.

The cloak that covers Procris's hips is an intense red, the triumphal color of alchemy. The dog sitting at her feet is also reddish in color, formally representing the *Canis Laelaps* that Diana gave to the nymph. In occultist alchemical texts, however, the dog symbolizes Hermes Trismegistus, the god of ancestral wisdom and thaumaturgical power. This dog appears twice in the painting: on the meadow in the foreground and again on the beach, where it faces the white dog and black cat—white and black being the other two magical colors of alchemy. These animals appear timid and submissive in the presence of their haughty companion, signifying that the alchemical arts are subject to the superior will of Hermes.

The birds in the background of *The Death of Procris* also represent various principles of alchemy. Those flying in the sky symbolize the sublimation of the volatile substances that the alchemist processes in his alembic, and those standing on the soil represent the substances that condense. In Piero di Cosimo's painting, a few herons can be seen on the shore; for the Egyptians, these symbolized the light of the sun, the eye of Ra that sees everything. In the distance, on the water, it is possible to distinguish some swans, representing the philosophical mercury: the alchemical work's mystical center through which is obtained the union of opposites.

The birds standing on the soil represent the all-seeing eye of Ra.

Another proof that Piero di Cosimo's painting has a close and occult relationship to alchemy is the winding path through the sand, scattered with stones. The painter intended to show the path of the alchemist's search, which changes direction and overcomes obstacles to reach his destiny. At the end of this path there is a pelican, clearly recognizable as a more detailed figure than the other birds. In alchemical treatises the pelican is the symbol for the philosopher's stone because this stone reproduces itself with its own energy, just like the bird, which was believed to feed its young with its own blood.

A Mysterious Artist

Piero di Cosimo's real name was Piero di Lorenzo; from the time of his youth he took the name of his master, Cosimo Rosselli, a mediocre painter, although of a certain renown. In 1480, Rosselli was called to work on the side panels of the Sistine Chapel along with great artists such as Botticelli, Perugino, and Ghirlandaio, and he took his apprentice with him. There, Piero painted the panel of the Sermon on the Mount and some other minor details, beginning his artistic career as the author of religious and secular works. Although his skills were only

Piero di Cosimo had a Hermetic and macabre imagination and knew well the secrets of alchemy.

average in this era of great geniuses, he succeeded in giving a mysterious luminosity to his mystical themes and a striking Tenebrism to his secular paintings. The painter and architect Giorgio Vasari described him as "a man of unpredictable humor, capable of very strange inventions."

Not much is known of Piero di Cosimo's private life, perhaps because his unsociable character caused him to live in solitude, removed from artistic circles and worldly interactions. The majority of his commissions were private and he is not known to have had apprentices or helpers, with the exception of Andrea del Sarto and possibly some collaboration with Ghirlandaio. The works of his lunatic and macabre imagination often included dragons, fauns, and fantastical beasts painted in his own particular style. It has been said that his master, Rosselli, practiced alchemy and passed its mysteries to Piero di Cosimo, who, if he was not an alchemist himself, at least knew very well the secrets of this occult science.

LEONARDO DA VINCI
THE LAST SUPPER
(1496–98)

This magnificent painting by the Italian artist (now in Santa Maria delle Grazie, Milan) is an encoded compendium of Christian esotericism: Jesus is not a divine being, and his brother and lover are hiding in the figures of two apostles while Leonardo da Vinci himself turns his back on the Master. (See color plates 6–7.)

The Great Fresco of Christian Heterodoxy

The Last Supper together with the *Mona Lisa* are Leonardo da Vinci's most admired known works. In *The Last Supper,* the great Renaissance master created a gestalt in which creativity, artistic talent, and technical innovation unite to express the perfection of the dramatic quality of this episode in the gospel. At the same time, it offers the initiate numerous symbols of occult significations connected with esoteric Christology. The work thus presents a bold and reformist vision to the religious paintings of the era, along with a cryptic message inspired by the gnostic gospels and the legend of the Holy Grail.

Leonardo chose to depict the moment at which Jesus spoke to his apostles the famous premonitory phrase: "One of you shall betray me." The Redeemer looks hurt but serene while the twelve apostles react with different attitudes: surprise, incredulity, pain, fear, and more subtle emotions. As a whole they present a horizontal movement, almost as if in a frieze, supported by the long table that conceals the characters from the waist down, except for a few feet that are only just visible beneath the table. Jesus' axial position is emphasized by the centralized vanishing point and the window behind him, which frames him in a bright landscape.

The first detail that draws the attention of the undoubtedly surprised viewer is the total absence of occipital auras distinguishing divine and holy figures. Neither Jesus nor the twelve apostles (all saints, except for one) have this golden halo—a serious defiance of the canons of religious painting. A second fact is the absence of the famous Grail or eucharistic chalice. It is neither visible on the table nor in Jesus' open hands nor in the hands of any of the apostles nor even on the floor. This cannot possibly be an error or oversight on the part of the artist, who was an obsessive perfectionist in every detail of his works.

According to most interpretations, this is a protest by omission, undoubtedly an intentional irreverence. Leonardo did not believe in the divinity of Jesus, did not accept the sanctity of the apostles, and did not partake in the miracle of the Eucharist. His Grail contained not wine transubstantiated into blood but the essential Hermetic secret guarded successively by the Essenes, the gnostics, and the Cathars.

Besides this noticeable absence, the esoteric reading of the painting presents a series of occult symbols and codes that have wracked the brains of its interpreters. The format of the work is greatly elongated; it covers an entire wall in the refectory of the convent of Santa Maria delle Grazie. The silhouette of Jesus forms an equilateral triangle on each side of which are two groups of three apostles each. All are showing their reactions to the tragic announcement, and each group has its own particular esoteric significance.

Nothing Is as It Seems

Beginning our interpretation from right to left, in the direction in which Leonardo da Vinci wrote, we see Simon, Jude Thaddeus (the "good" Judas), and Matthew, who receive the news with an air of confusion. We can note, though, that the face of the Jude Thaddeus is an unmistakable self-portrait of Leonardo himself. The artist also has his back turned to the Master, as does Matthew, the most heterodox Evangelist. The gestures of both appear to express "Why is he saying this?" while Simon opens his hands as if to say he doesn't understand either. The second trio is composed of Philip, author of one of the gnostic gospels; an astonished James the Greater; and the incredulous

Jude Thaddeus is in fact Leonardo da Vinci himself.

Thomas, raising his finger to make a Hermetic sign that we will explore shortly. Curiously, of the six apostles on the right side, only Philip is looking attentively at Jesus.

The group on the far left is composed of Bartholomew, James the Less, and Andrew. The three show surprise, in keeping with the tradition of previous painters of the Last Supper. But Leonardo presented an essential enigma in the figure of the young James: His hair, profile, and tunic are exact copies of the Redeemer's in the painting. With what intent did Leonardo place this double of Jesus at the table of *The Last Supper?* The explanation that receives the greatest consensus from the experts is that James the Less was Jesus' twin or younger brother, as mentioned in the gnostic gospels and Arabic sources; in fact, the Gospel of John calls him Didymus, meaning "twin." This clone of the Messiah supposedly took Jesus' place in public appearances, and perhaps it was he who died on the cross.

*James the Less, allegedly Jesus'
twin, according to Hermetic
tradition took Jesus' place at
the crucifixion.*

A Woman among the Apostles

In the three figures just to the left of Jesus, leaning between Andrew
and Jesus, Leonardo brought together the most significant symbols
in Christian Hermeticism. These are Judas Iscariot (the villain of the
canonical gospels), Peter, and John. Various exegetes have pointed out
that the image of this last, the "most beloved disciple," exhibits feminine features typical in Leonardo's paintings—and it does appear so.
His complexion is much lighter than those of the other figures. (See
plate 6.) Yet, though John was young and sensitive, he was not effemi-
nate, at least according to known sources. Further, if this is John, there
is no justification for his privileged placement at Jesus' right side, where
Peter, the senior member and chief of the apostles, should be.

If we accept that this is not John but a female figure, however,
we must wonder who it is. There were no women among the apostles,
but the woman seated among them, in the most prominent position,

must be someone very close to Jesus. It cannot be his mother, Mary, because the mysterious supper companion appears even younger than the Messiah himself. Who could it be, then? The answer is obvious for those initiated into esoteric Christology: Mary Magdalene, the repentant sinner who was the lover and possibly the wife of Jesus and who may have carried in her womb the seed of the sacred lineage of the Royal Blood.

The Announcement of a Crime

In the same group, Leonardo presented the most tragic and heretical symbol included in *The Last Supper* with elements that would have been obvious to the public. Peter leans toward Mary Magdalene with a threatening expression while his left hand makes a cutting gesture over the young woman's throat. In his right hand he holds a knife, hidden behind Judas's back. In any secular painting, a person with this posture would be seen clearly as an assassin about to commit his crime. Yet neither Ludovico il Moro, who commissioned the work, nor the mistrustful Holy Office, nor the monks of the Church of Santa Maria delle Grazie noticed the tremendous significance of this scene. This may have been because this brutal deed and the audacity of describing it were totally unthinkable but also because Leonardo skillfully manipulated his painting to make the visible invisible.

The sinister gesture of Peter's left hand appears concealed by the left hand of James the Less, which is placed upon Peter's shoulder. Both Peter's and James's forefingers appear to point to Jesus in an innocent gesture, but in fact Peter is pointing to the place where he will drive his knife into Mary's throat while the Master's "double" (James) attempts to take Peter's arm to stop him. The position of Peter's right arm is strangely forced, so that the hand that holds the weapon appears to hang in the air, as if it is ready to slice a piece from a plate of meat— or as if it belonged to someone else who stoops hidden behind Judas. Leonardo completed the visual trick by painting a small knife that blends in with the background colors.

What reason could the leader of the apostles have had for assassinating Mary Magdalene? As in so many other cases, this crime would have been committed in order to obtain power. The Messiah had announced: "One of you shall betray me," and this meant Jesus would be judged and condemned to a long imprisonment or even to death. Someone must be his successor, and the logical candidate had always been Peter, the first of the apostles, the one to whom was given the assignment to found the future Christian Church. As depicted here, however, Jesus brings Mary Magdalene to supper and places her to his right. Somehow, he may have indicated her as his heiress, or perhaps he announced it moments before the time depicted in the painting, and Peter is seized by jealousy and resentment. The gnostic evangelists, especially Philip, speak of a constant animosity between Peter and Mary, suggesting that they envied each other's respective influences over the Master. The assassin's posture given the apostle by Leonardo is undoubtedly symbolic and was perhaps intended to state clearly to initiates that this version of *The Last Supper* was faithful to the gnostic heterodoxy.

The Invisible Grail

Leonardo da Vinci's most mysterious and transcendental message is not in any element of the painting but rather in a detail missing from it. Along with the triangle with its vertices at Jesus' head and hands, another inverted triangle is formed by the arms of the Master and Mary Magdalene. If we continue this triangle to the windows in the background, we can trace the outline of a cup or chalice, or at least this is seen by those initiated into Christological Mysteries. This hidden chalice is the Grail that does not appear on the table; it is invisible because it is an immaterial symbol. Outlined and supported by the couple, this Grail also represents the womb of Mary Magdalene consecrated by Jesus' seed, which began the lineage of the Royal Blood.

With this cryptic message, Leonardo declared his adherence to the most esoteric Christology, confirmed by his irreverent self-portrait in

Jude Thaddeus and the symbols already mentioned relating to Jesus' twin, the initiatory gesture of Thomas's finger, and Peter's criminal posture toward Mary Magdalene. The whole painting is in fact a kind of heterodox "catechism," leaving no doubt as to the author's inclination toward Hermetic knowledge.

A Man of His Time

Leonardo da Vinci is considered the archetypal Renaissance man, and as such, he was a scholar and practitioner of all the arts and sciences of his era. He was a brilliant painter, sculptor, engraver, and architect; he made important discoveries in anatomy and in the realm of nature; he foresaw and tested advances in mechanics, aviation, and transportation; and he built machines for working and measuring. His mind attempted to embrace all wisdom at a time when alchemy and astrology were integral parts of it. He also mingled with the intellectuals and philosophers of Renaissance Florence, mistrustful of ecclesiastic doctrine and greatly influenced by the rediscovery of Plato, Pythagoras, and other heterodox thinkers from Greece and Byzantium. These Renaissance

Leonardo's self-portrait drawn in 1516, three years before his death

men questioned the Vatican's manipulations and concealments of the truth of the gospels and the authentic history and preaching of Jesus of Nazareth. Leonardo da Vinci's cryptic message was intended not only for those contemporary initiates but also for the preservation in works of art of the esoteric mysteries and the secret of the Royal Blood.

In the controversial *Prieuré Documents* kept at the Bibliothèque Nationale in Paris, Leonardo is mentioned as grand master of the Priory of Sion between 1510 and 1519, after Botticelli, and he was supposedly succeeded by the constable of Bourbon. This list of the grand masters was "retrieved" and published in 1981 by a dubious personality named Pierre Plantard, and the very existence of the Priory lacks the historical consistency of the Order of the Temple, Catharism, or Masonry. Despite this, secret societies and sects were certainly abundant in Italy in the early sixteenth century and it is probable that Leonardo, like many artists and intellectuals, belonged to some of them.

This is confirmed by the enigmatic sign made by Thomas in *The Last Supper:* His fist is closed and his index finger is raised vertically. This gesture appears for the first time in Leonardo's work *Adoration of the Magi* (1481), in which John the Baptist's hand makes it from behind a tree—and it is repeated in the first version of *The Virgin of the Rocks,* on display in the Louvre. It is also present in the sketch for *Virgin and Child with St. Anne* and is very clear in *St. John the Baptist.* Because of this, it was known as the sign of John and was so typical of Leonardo that when the artist served as a model for Plato in Raphael's *School of Athens,* Raphael painted Leonardo da Vinci with his right arm raised and his hand making this same gesture.

John the Baptist was a recognized and highly influential Essene prophet whose declaration that Jesus was the Messiah was fundamental to the birth of Christianity. The majority of heterodox and gnostic beliefs used him as their principal reference, so it is not at all odd that the sign of John was used by the adherents of some of these teachings in order to recognize others who shared their beliefs. Leonardo included the gesture in his works as another message intended for the initiates of Christian esotericism.

The Mona Lisa's *Smile*

It is common enough for artists' guides and manuals to say that Leonardo's *Mona Lisa* has a suggestive and mysterious smile. This much is an obvious truth, but the strange fascination commanded by this feminine portrait is not limited to her expression. Even more famous than *The Last Supper*, it is a small painting, about 30 x 21 inches, and is on display at the Louvre Museum in Paris, where it is protected by sophisticated security measures. (It was stolen in 1911 and recovered two years later in Florence.) The viewer who manages to navigate the captivated and ever-replenishing crowd in front of the painting will feel immediately moved by the inexplicable magic that emanates from the face of this young Renaissance woman.

The first impression of the work is that the portrait transforms into a living being before our eyes. The subject's expression changes with each angle, smiling alternately placidly and sadly, and her eyes gently follow our movements. The thought about this painting is that Leonardo da Vinci did not merely paint a portrait of this Florentine woman but that his brushes performed a miracle, keeping her alive forever. In this work there are no Hermetic symbols or coded messages for initiates; its message goes beyond esotericism. It casts a spell that makes art a bridge leading to the mystery of life and death.

Perhaps inspired by the numen of the god Trismegistus, Leonardo applied extraordinary creative wisdom and many pictorial devices in the *Mona Lisa* that together were worthy of the thaumaturge he truly was. The painting conceals an astonishing trick: Its two halves are not symmetrical. This difference is more obvious in the mountainous landscape that occupies the background: The horizon on the left is significantly lower than that on the right. The result is that, depending on the side from which we view the painting, its subject appears higher or lower to us, and if we move, she appears to raise or lower her head softly.

The Mona Lisa. *The portrait transforms itself from every viewpoint; her smile can be placid or sad and her eyes follow our movements. Leonardo da Vinci's genius gave life to this portrait and made a bridge of art that leads to the mystery of life and death.*

The same asymmetry is present in Mona Lisa's face, causing apparent changes in her features and smiling lips as we adjust our point of view. The sensation that the artist has breathed life into the portrait is completed by the use of sfumato, a laborious technique invented by Leonardo himself that consists of overlaying light brush strokes in distinct shades. Using this method, he blurred the strokes of the paintbrush on the face and hands, making the model's skin softer and more delicate.

Since the time of this portrait's creation, hundreds of portrait artists, some of them very talented in their own way, have tried to repeat the miracle. Nevertheless, five centuries later, only the *Mona Lisa* lives on, smiling at us with definite smugness behind the thick glass that protects her in the Louvre.

HIERONYMUS BOSCH
THE GARDEN OF EARTHLY DELIGHTS
(ca. 1504)

The Flemish master Bosch painted numerous gnostic symbols into his works, which depict the world as a satanic creation in keeping with the mysterious legacy of the last remaining Cathars. (See color plate 5.)

An Unrepentant World Created by Satan

The name Hieronymus Bosch brings to mind a horrific pictorial universe, strange and unique amid the art of the late fifteenth and early sixteenth centuries. His works tend to show different scenes with no congruence to one another and intentionally exhibit disdain for the rules of nature and geography. The typology of the people—or rather, the creatures—that populate his paintings is at once varied and repetitious, its range including the heavenly, the earthly, and the monstrous. Devils, owls, monkeys, anthropomorphic fish, and fantastical animals mingle with naked women, bishops, musicians, beggars, nuns, cripples, children, old people, and figures that combine human aspects and those that are zoological or even vegetable. The many scenes and situations contained within each painting or triptych exhibit satirical motifs of eroticism and violence, along with allusions to the deadly sins and the ignominies and miseries of earthly life.

Even the most uninformed observer of art can see that Bosch's paintings demand interpretation, that his marvelous dreamlike colors conceal an intentional message for the initiated. An initial exegesis finds, in his surreal and deliberately absurd subject matter, a comic denunciation of the abuses of the Church and aristocracy, the coarseness of the masses, the vices of all people, and the general decadence of spiritual values and ethics. This moralizing intent is indisputably obvious in his paintings, but present also is a secret substratum which alludes to more transcendent esoteric concepts. These Hermetic allusions occur in all the artist's major works. Let us begin by searching for them in what is perhaps the most famous and the most cryptic of his works: *The Garden of Earthly Delights,* now at the Prado Museum in Madrid.

A Depiction of the Carnal Sins

Hieronymus Bosch painted the triptych *The Garden of Earthly Delights* in oil around the beginning of the sixteenth century, probably in 1504. The center panel is a multicolored painting, approximately 87 x 49 inches; the side panels are the same height, 87 inches, with a width of about 38 inches. As in other triptychs, the left panel represents heaven, the right hell. The center panel, however, the source of the work's fame, shows a great number of peculiar scenes, most of them featuring naked people. Although some of the characters' activities border on the obscene, they convey not a pleasant eroticism but

A beautiful depiction of the ugly: The center panel, from which this detail comes, is a great scene showing a world that, although fantastical, is still earthly—our real world as a diabolical creation.

instead an intentional asexuality. It is as if the artist wished not to praise corporeal beauty and sensual enjoyment, but rather to expose the physical and spiritual misery of carnal sins.

The center panel has three distinct horizontal sections that are clearly divided from one another by two strips of hedge or bushes running from one side of the panel to the other. In the lower third of the painting, the naked figures are closer to the observer and are involved in various erotic games—including zoophilia, cunnilingus, and sadism—amid enormous strawberries and currants, dead fish, and outlandish objects with obscure symbolism. In this section we can notice the inclusion of a black couple: The woman is located at the far left and the man at the far right, and each has a great cherry on her or his head. In addition, we can see that two characters are sticking their heads out of giant eggs, one to kiss a man and the other to kiss a bird resembling a raven. Higher up on the left, close to the upper limit of this area, we see the shore of a lake from which are springing forth several enormous birds. Near this are a number of scenes of a dream-like character in which more naked characters, continuing their lewd actions, peek out of gigantic fruits or are covered by transparent spheres or domes.

The central third of the panel is a grassy meadow with a pond in the middle wherein are bathing a number of young people—naturally, also nude. Around them parades a cavalcade of naked riders mounting all manner of quadrupeds, including a few horses. On each side of the pond and parade are additional scenes, more difficult to interpret, in which groups of nudists interact with fantastical beings or objects.

Finally, in the upper third of the panel, five great structures appear. These could be fortresses or castles invented by an architect gone mad. From the bases of the two central structures, two streams run and flow into a river. In this river there floats what appears to be a metallic sphere, which supports a strange column adorned with exotic fruits. The structures are made of materials that resemble parts of vegetables and bits of crustaceans, and in all of them we can see tiny naked people.

A strange metallic sphere adorned with exotic fruits floats on a river in the upper third of the center panel.

Scholars have identified more than fifty principal themes in *The Garden of Earthly Delights,* aside from the subtopics and isolated figures peppering the entire surface of the painting. In every scene in this exuberant imagery, Bosch achieved a striking effect, connecting all its significance to that of the rest of the work. The painting shows a world, which, although fantastical, is still earthly: our real world as a diabolical creation. This idea that the creator was not God but Satan was the basis of the cosmogony of certain gnostic movements, particularly medieval Catharism.

The Last Cathar?

The British scholar Linda Harris, who dedicated fifteen years to studying the work of Hieronymus Bosch, has recently claimed the truth of his alleged Catharism. The Cathars, whose main center was medieval France, were suppressed in 1207 and were eliminated soon afterward in a brutal extermination. Their religion, however, survived in an underground form in other regions, including Lombardy, the Veneto, and the Balkans. Further, although three hundred years is a long time, Harris claims that in the early sixteenth century, Bosch was a kind of secret Cathar. Other authors have concurred in doubting the Catholicism of this Flemish master, who was indeed a gnostic and was staunchly anticlerical and had connections to the pantheistic Brotherhood of the Free Spirit, a heretical sect that celebrated and enjoyed the pleasures of the world and the flesh that the Church condemned. Yet this hedonistic heresy appears opposed to the vision Hieronymus Bosch shows in his work, especially in *The Garden of Earthly Delights,* a caustic critique of unrestrained, bestial sensuality.

Linda Harris supports her claim in this contradiction by stating that Bosch's paintings are allegories of the world that surrounded him. A perverted and unrepentant world could only be a satanic invention—and it was the Cathars who claimed that the terrestrial world was the devil's creation. Harris points out that the painter traveled to Venice and Bosnia in order to contact secret Cathars and that his connection to the strictly Catholic Brotherhood of Our Lady and the highly pagan Brotherhood of the Free Spirit were both deceptions arranged in order to hide his true dualistic beliefs.

The Garden of Earthly Delights is the main proof for claiming Bosch's adherence to secret, surviving Catharism (and active neo-Cathar groups that exist even today). This interpretation begins with the sides of the triptych: In the left panel there is a suspicious Paradise in which Jesus, holding Eve's hand, could be either the Savior who redeems her from her sins or the disguised devil who leads her to commit them. An owl—a creature with satanic associations both in medieval sorcery and in Flemish art—is hiding in the fountain, cryptically confirming the gnostic and Cathar theogony that considers the incarnation of Jesus to be a trick played by the devil. Further, the hell depicted in the right panel does not seem to be the Christian hell. Rather, it is earth after the extinction of Catharism—an earth converted into a terrible underworld of unrepentant beings who are condemned for the delights offered by their diabolical creator.

The lavish scene in the center panel, displaying Bosch's inexhaustible imagination for conceiving fantastic images, thus illustrates the message contained in the side panels: The terrestrial world is a satanic creation devised by an evil creator. This creator even incarnated himself as a false redeemer in order to conceal from us the true path to salvation, which was the absolute individual purity that was accessible only to the initiates of gnostic Catharism.

An Esoteric Moralist

The hypothesis of Hieronymus Bosch's Catharism is undoubtedly interesting, but in the field of academic iconography there is still reluctance to accept it as proven fact. What is certain is that the great Flemish master, whether or not he belonged to this supposedly vanished religion, created a project of esoteric symbolism in order to chastise our demonic world and draw attention to spiritual and moral values. With its occult symbols, his art was intended to convey an attitude of purity and mysticism that was on the way to extinction in order to hand down these symbols to the posterity that would be able to read them. This viewpoint coincided with that of many of his educated countrymen in an era of rising Hermeticism and dislike of the Catholic Church that was forming a breeding ground for the imminent Lutheran reform. The presence of a number of gnostic symbols and messages is obvious in Bosch's work, not only in *The Garden of Earthly Delights* but also in other significant paintings.

The Haywain, painted a few years earlier, appears to be the illustration of a Flemish proverb: "The world is a haystack, and each man plucks from it what he can." It is also a triptych, with its center panel depicting an immense wagon that is overloaded with hay and is drawn by Bosch's usual monstrous creatures. Atop the mountain of dried grass in the wagon there takes place an apparently idyllic scene: A pale lute player strums a musical score held in the hands of a woman who wears a serene expression. A third person crouches behind them, guiding the reading with his finger, and these three people are flanked by an angel in ecstasy and a demon playing a bagpipe chanter, a phallic symbol in medieval imagery. Behind this group is a large shrub with a couple kissing within its foliage, and behind the shrub is a man spying on the couple. Thus the placid calm of the trio and their melodic music is disturbed by

A wagon doomed to condemnation in The Haywain. *The artist depicts the terrestrial world as a den of rapacious and egotistical sinners, devoid of spiritual concern.*

the sound of the satanic bagpipe chanter and is unseen by the sinning couple and the observer watching them. Protruding from the shrub is a solitary branch on which is perched the ubiquitous owl.

Behind the hay wagon there is a procession, headed by the pope, emperor, and king, who lead a diverse entourage, as if the rulers were following the unavoidable destiny of the wagon, which is pulled toward hell by various demons. Beneath and between the wheels of the wagon groups of men, women, and friars fight each other to grab bunches of hay, using ladders, pitchforks, hooks, and their bare hands. These include one man who is cutting another's throat upon the arid, dry soil. In the lower part of the panel there unfold various scenes, including that of a peddler with two children, who probably have been kidnapped, and a cryptic scene with three women and their respective children (or perhaps the same woman and child seen three times). In this depiction, one child is pulling on a woman's skirt, one is wrapped in a woman's shawl, and the third is having his rear end washed by another woman. To the right of this there is a dentist with his tools stuck in a woman's mouth. At the far right, some nuns, directed by an obese monk holding a glass of wine, fill a bag with stolen hay, while another nun steals a bag from a strange piper clad in green.

In *The Haywain* Bosch again depicted the terrestrial world as a den of rapacious and egotistical sinners devoid of spiritual concern. In this work, this vision is emphasized by the inclusion at the top of the painting of a small Christ on a cloud, who appears to bless the entire scene. His partially naked and suspiciously androgynous body is covered only by the loincloth of the crucifixion and the red cloak of the Redeemer, while his ambiguous face is beardless and the dubious halo behind his head is barely perceptible. In him Bosch painted a small and distant Jesus with a childlike face and indefinite gender who makes an uncertain gesture, perhaps to say that this was the best Golem the devil could manage to create and pass off as the Lord incarnate.

HANS BALDUNG
THE THREE AGES OF THE WOMAN AND DEATH
(ca. 1510)

This painting by Baldung, now in the Kunsthistorisches Museum in Vienna, is considered archetypal of the Tenebrist genre and depicts an eerie encounter between the macabre and the sensual in which symbolic and esoteric messages are presented with intentional ambiguity. (See color plate 8.)

A Macabre and Ambiguous Enigma

Like other works by this strange German artist, *The Three Ages of the Woman and Death* emanates a sexuality that is dismal and erotic at the same time. Its current title is a convention and is based on the common trend at the time for depicting the ages of human life. The painter never acknowledged this was his topic, nor did he bother to deny it. The Viennese museum where the painting is kept named it *Allegory of the Ephemeral* in 1938. Twenty years later the name was changed to *The Three Ages of the Woman and Death,* and at some traveling exhibitions it has been presented as the *Allegory of Earthly Vanity* or, less imaginatively, as *Beauty and Death.* This title uncertainty of curators and experts points to the thematic ambiguity of the artist, who left posterity a masterpiece combined with a controversial enigma.

The scene in the painting shows four figures, all standing almost vertically in a clearing in a dark forest. The character occupying most of the right half of the canvas is surely the symbol of Death as the German Renaissance masters tended to depict him. In this case, however, he is not the usual animated skeleton, but instead is a kind of repulsive zombie, his flesh falling away in tatters. The other figure who stands out is a beautiful young woman who is entirely naked (except for the indispensable and opportunely placed veil covering her loins), looking absorbedly at herself in a hand mirror, indifferent to what is happening behind her back. There, a manly-looking old woman is shown entering the scene wearing a tense and agitated expression. At the feet of the two women, in the lower part of the left section of the painting, a child kneels, almost completely covered by the aforementioned veil.

We can note a strangely forced position and some errors of proportion in the left arms of the three standing figures and in the child's left leg, but these should not be attributed to the artist's ineptitude. As can be seen in the rest of the painting, and particularly in the young woman, Baldung had a masterful command of human anatomy. This distortion of forms was surely deliberate, a kind of personal mark that distinguished him from his contemporaries in the same school.

Pressing in closely around all the characters is the wooded background and, behind it, a grayish sky. The foliage is not green, but an earthy brown, though it lightens a bit around the young woman. This vegetation disappears altogether in the area near Death, however; taking its place is a truncated tree overgrown with yellowish grasses and parasitic fungi that clings to the flaking bark. The undergrowth beneath the figures' feet includes a ripe fruit at the foot of the child and a few plant shoots budding between and near the young woman's ankles—though these fade away beneath the feet of Death.

More than Just Symbolic Figures

The work's execution is excellent, but it cannot be said that its theme is agreeable. It is undoubtedly part of the Tenebrist movement of the German Renaissance that was dedicated to showing feminine beauty juxtaposed with Dantean images denouncing its vanity and the ephemeral nature of its brilliance. In order to express this, a beautiful young woman—who might be the goddess Venus—was often painted along with a macabre figure symbolizing death, usually a fleshless skeleton. An initial interpretation of *The Three Ages of the Woman and Death* might attribute this painting to this genre of the epoch's art. Baldung, however, had too feverish and devious an imagination to limit himself to painting simply another version of what had already been created.

Various possible keys to the work's symbolism can be found in the left side of the canvas—perhaps preferred by the artist because the word *left* is associated with *sinister.* In the upper left corner we see the arm of Death raised and holding an hourglass over the young woman's head. Behind her head the old woman's hand attempts to ward off this gesture. We can also notice that this old woman, wrinkled and tooth-less, has an air of concerned decisiveness that lends a certain nobility. It is not entirely clear, however, whether this is an old woman or a man. Her left breast, which can be seen between the young woman's hair and mirror, could also be part of a man's torso deformed by the black rectangle that also distorts the profile of her side and thigh. This ambiguous character is entering the painting from the left side, and the truncation of this side prevents us from seeing its genital area.

This revealing upper left corner of the canvas also shows that the mirror in which the young woman is contemplating her beauty is made of convex crystal. In an era when flat crystals were used as mirrors, only witchcraft preserved the medieval tradition of using a convex mir-ror for certain spells. Undoubtedly, the great initiate Hans Baldung knew this. Another gender ambiguity presented by the painting can be found in the figure of the infant that appears in the lower left cor-ner. We might suppose that this figure is the woman in her childhood, but some sharp-eyed experts have distinguished male genitalia behind the covering veil. If the child is a boy, as the wooden rocking horse at "his" feet might suggest, then the whole theory of the painting present-ing the three ages is overturned, and Baldung's interpreters are back at square one.

Gender Ambiguity

One rather strange interpretation proposes that the ages of life are united by the veil that almost completely covers the child (an allusion to the uterus?), wraps around the young woman and covers her loins, and is held by the figure on the right, who is a hybrid between Old Age and Death. From there, the translucent fabric continues downward—in Baldung's view, probably toward hell. Aside from the obvious attributes

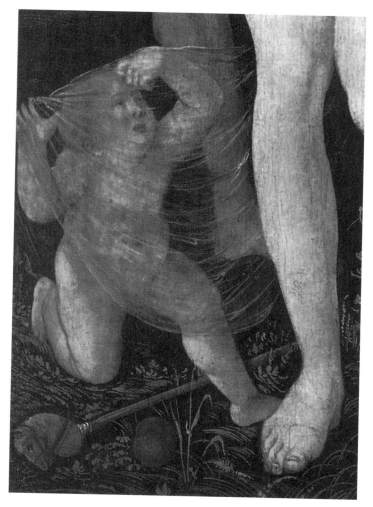

The gender of the child at the young woman's feet cannot be precisely determined, although some shadows in the veil suggest it might be a boy.

of the young woman, the gender of each of the other two characters in this trilogy is not very clear, although it could be accepted that they are female. It is also plausible that Old Age is brandishing the hourglass in order to remind Youth of the passing of time and that, enthralled by fatuous pride in her beauty, Youth does not notice it.

What does not fit into this explanation of the work's symbolism is

*The young woman holds back her beautiful hair with one hand while with the
other she holds the mirror typical of allegories of vanity.*

the presence and attitude of the fourth character: an older person who
hastens to halt the passage of time and the onset of old age. One variation in interpretation suggests that in fact there are depicted here not
three ages but four, considering that this division was not clear-cut in
the imagery of the era and that another work by the same artist is entitled *The Seven Ages of Woman.* Perhaps what Baldung really wanted to
depict was an *Allegory of the Ephemeral,* as stated in one of the painting's alternate, previous titles: The child arrives in this world already
enveloped in the veil of Death; vain, beautiful Youth rejects the passage
of time and here turns toward the mirror; and Death holds Youth with
his veil in order to take her with him when her time comes.

In this version, the fourth figure who tries to halt this process
once again has an unclear identity. Some have seen her as Old Age
resisting Death; some have claimed that she is a witch or sorcerer
who opposes Death with a magic spell or that she is an emanation of
ancestral wisdom—Hermetic knowledge, capable of altering the laws
of nature.

The Cipher of the Universe

Some scholars of Hans Baldung's esoteric side claim that whoever may be the characters in *The Three Ages of the Woman and Death,* their number and positioning transmits a hidden message to the eye. With their admiration of classical Greece, the thinkers and artists of the Renaissance revolutionized, among many things, Pythagorean numerology. The great master of Samos claimed that true knowledge could be attained only by way of mathematics and that every number was a cipher that carried within it a key for decoding the world. Although absolute wisdom, or the cipher of the universe, was never found, this view maintains that certain combinations of numbers produce a mysterious power that enlightens the mind and reveals aspects of occult knowledge.

Baldung placed the figures in his painting in one group of three and a group of one—with the one being either the young woman, distinguished by her paleness and beauty, or Death, being in a different position, facing the others. In the traditional texts of numerology, the numeral 1 represents primordial unity, the initial impulse of Creation. Three is a prime number in the ordinal series, a symbol of the trinitarian Egyptian and Hindu deities and the Christian Trinity. It symbolizes creative power, destructive power, and the equilibrium between the two. The sum of the characters (1 + 3) is 4, a numeral signifying the real and material part of the universe and also representing the magic square that the alchemists sought to integrate with the circle. If this interpretation seems unusual today, it would have been obvious to an educated person around 1500 with a general knowledge of numerology.

An Outlandish and Enigmatic Artist

Hans Baldung's prolific and diverse body of work is exhibited in prestigious museums all over the world and has been studied exhaustively by noted experts and critics. Whether these people agree in their interpretations of his paintings, drawings, and engravings, however, is another question. Born in 1484 in the small city of Gmünd, in what is now

Germany, Baldung was an apprentice in Dürer's studio along with Lucas Cranach, which has resulted in Cranach's and Baldung's works often being confused with each other or with these creations being attributed to Dürer, the master. Baldung soon distinguished himself, however, by cultivating a particular enthusiasm for macabre themes and bestowing a supernatural aura on his religious paintings. His greatest masterpiece is considered to be the *Coronation of the Virgin,* completed in 1516 for Freiburg Cathedral. This work emanates a mysterious luminosity that is truly celestial.

Baldung's broad artistic interests were not restricted to pious themes; they also embraced the mythological and the allegorical, the mysterious and the esoteric, although he did paint portraits on commission and designed stained-glass windows and tapestries. Despite his inclination toward the macabre, he tended to combine it with a lively and refined eroticism, a contrast between sensuality and putrefaction that lent an attractive turbidity to works such as *Woman and Death* and *The Three Graces*—and to the *The Three Ages of the Woman and Death* discussed here.

In this painting Baldung wove together such strands as these into a work that is exceptional in its artistic level and technical eccentricity and in the aura of mystery pervading it.

ALBRECHT DÜRER
MELANCHOLIA I
(1514)

In this engraving, now housed in Gabinetto dei Disegni e delle Stampe, Florence, Albrecht Dürer reflected the esoteric preoccupation with time and depicted a number of messages and symbols handed down from the magical occultism of the Middle Ages. (See color plate 9.)

The Legacy of Medieval Magic

Melancholia was believed to have been caused by an excess of black bile, or *melaina cholé,* one of the four humors that were believed to mark the characters of individuals in classical antiquity: In the sanguine or passionate red blood prevailed; the phlegmatic or impassive had a surplus of mucus or phlegm; and the choleric or irritable were said to have a great quantity of yellow bile (choler). It is no easy task to describe the character corresponding to the humor of melaina cholé.

Victor Hugo defined melancholia as "the enjoyment of being sad," and it is certain that this sentiment or state of mind is characterized by its unstable ambiguity. Yet since antiquity this condition has enjoyed an aura of distinction in philosophy as well as in poetry and art. Eighteenth-century Germans called it Werther's complaint, the nineteenth-century French called it *mal du siècle,* and the early twentieth-century English called it spleen.

Marsilio Ficino, the Renaissance thinker who delved into esoteric sources, said that melancholy was like the axis of the world and that it "drove the soul to seek the center of singular things"—that is, all things unique, marvelous, and occult. Perhaps this search was driving Dürer when, in 1513 and 1514, he created a number of beautiful engravings that are difficult to interpret: *Knight, Death, and the Devil; St. Jerome in His Cell;* and *Melancholia I.* This last is the richest in symbolic and enigmatic elements.

Ordered Disorder

The first impression produced by this magnificent engraving is one of a motley disorder. In it there are a great number of instruments and tools lying about, occupying all the available space, scattered here and there, even reaching beyond the edges of the scene. Among this profusion we can distinguish, with difficulty, a cherub and a dog. They accompany the central allegorical figure: a corpulent, seated angel, apparently female, occupying a large part of the right-hand section of the engraving. Above her head there appear some more ordered elements, and in the background to the left a rainbow forms around a diminutive sun, its rays shining on a calm sea.

The best method for analyzing such elements is to consider them one by one, according to their specific importance to the whole. The most notable image here is that of the melancholic angel dressed in a rich and heavy Venetian robe and holding a compass whose points are concealed by a fold of cloth. We might suppose that the points of the compass are resting on a geometric drawing or plan, also hidden on the angel's lap. This instrument of the compass may be a reference to the intellectual and creative component of melancholy, but also to its tendency toward inaction, for the angel is not using it or even looking at it. Her other arm supports her head, with its hand on her temple and its elbow on her knee in a classic gesture of reflection or dejection (once again, the ambiguity of melancholy, which might be defined as a contemplative sadness). Yet the angel's eyes do not show sorrow, but rather an intense, keen gaze directed at some point outside the space of the engraving. The figure wears a crown of laurel, a symbol of triumph and prestige, and on her back are angelic wings, which do not seem capable of taking flight, weighed by such complex and heavy garments. At the angel's feet there is a full moneybag, an allusion to mercantile success and the covetousness associated with bilious humor.

To the left of the melancholic central figure is a chubby little angel, fully clothed, seated on the edge of a millstone and concentrating very intently on what it is writing on a tablet held in its hand. According to

The small angel represents the philosophical aspect associated with the melancholic character.

scholars of Dürer's work, this figure symbolizes the philosophical tendency attributed to melancholics. The third living being in the engraving is a dog with a goatlike head that is curled in a forced position on the left side of the image. This animal is the only element that is repeated in the three engravings of the series, and its significance tends to be associated with faithfulness and alertness to danger. In front of the dog there is a sphere and behind it a polyhedron, symbols of magical Pythagorean geometry. The ladder visible in the background, besides being a Masonic symbol, represents ascent to a higher dimension, a transcendent ability for which melancholics were thought to yearn.

On the ground lie a number of artisan's tools, which have been apparently abandoned by the angel of melancholy, whom Dürer depicted in a pensive moment of ambivalence between action and reflection. Barely visible behind the great polyhedron is a small cauldron on a fire, the artist's obvious homage to alchemy.

Time and the Kabbalah

The setting for this scene is a kind of terrace or balcony partly closed off by a wall. Hanging on this wall are a few significant objects that symbolize the principal concepts related to melancholy. Those with this humor were thought not to deal well with the passage of time, which overwhelmed the sensitive spirits of the Renaissance. Thus Dürer's angel keeps time locked inside a large and luxurious hourglass, which she controls with a hand bell used for marking the hours.

According to the numerology of Pythagoras and the medieval kabbalists, numerals and their combinations contain all the mysteries and secrets of the universe. One method for revealing them is to compose a *tabula Iovis* (table of Jupiter) or magic square, divided into equal cells with each one containing a number. The sum of the numbers along a vertical, horizontal, or diagonal line must always be the same. This esoteric invention was revived in the second half of the fifteenth century, and one of these squares is depicted in this engraving, hanging on the wall below the bell. In this case, there are sixteen cells, four on each side, and the magical result is 34. Dürer placed the numerals 15 and 14 in the bottom row, and together they form 1514, the year in which this work was executed—but this was also the date of the death of his mother, to whom the artist was very close. Perhaps this ill-fated event led Dürer to capture his own melancholy with his engraving tool and carve the sorrowful confusion caused by pitiless time.

This detail shows the table of Jupiter, a clear numerological and kabbalistic symbol.

A Peaceful Evening

Finally, there is the panorama in the background of the engraving, which shows a village (framed, incidentally, in a square formed by rungs of the ladder) on a mountainous coast next to a perfectly tranquil sea. The setting sun's rays form a clear rainbow, which may be a reference to what Dürer was experiencing: His mother had just died, and this shining rainbow above a serene landscape might signify the gentle relief of death after the torment of life. Another interpretation, which does not exclude the previous one, proposes that this placid yet resplendent background may represent the mental duality of the melancholic humor.

The curve of the rainbow encloses both the title of the engraving and the sun itself. Although this sun is small, its light spreads with considerable force, as if the light radiates from a cosmic explosion or announces a celestial apparition. Thus it is a powerful and extraterrestrial force, moving to oppose the immobility that reigns in the foreground of the engraving. The very title of the work appears to confirm this symbolism, for there never was a *Melancholia II,* nor is it known whether Dürer had a sequel in mind. This *I* therefore may not be a Roman number, but the Latin word *i,* second person singular imperative of the verb *eo,* meaning "go." This creation, then, is not just an allegorical engraving of melancholy, but also a magical incantation for dispelling this humor from the artist's spirit.

The letters of the title are written on the spread wings of a kind of giant bat whose eyes and mouth express an almost supernatural suffering. The artist did not include the creature's rear legs, but he did give it a strange, serpentine tail, making it a dragonlike creature, a nightmarish monster that appears to have sprung from magical medieval imagery. This creature is yet another symbol revealing that *Melancholia I* is above all a testimony to the persistence of witchcraft, even under the skeptical light of the Renaissance.

TITIAN
SACRED AND PROFANE LOVE
(1515–16)

In this early work now in the Borghese Gallery in Rome, the great Venetian master painted an unusual and Hermetic version of the two opposing forms of love using pagan symbols and alchemical colors. (See color plates 10–11.)

Naked Beauty as the Path to Perfection

This beautiful and colorful work, painted by Tiziano Vecellio (Titian) at the age of twenty-five, is one of the paintings that is most representative of the Neoplatonic symbolism cultivated by the circles the young painter frequented. This esoteric and mythological ideology upholds the famous Hermetic maxim, "as above, so below," and thus contemplation of the beauty of Creation permits a perception of the divine perfection of the universe. The art of adepts of this ideology had to be earthly, for its mystique was not in the idealized stylization of heavenly figures and scenes, but rather in the faithful depiction of the most beautiful aspects of nature.

In the symbolization of the two aspects of love in this work, Titian conveyed a heterodox and pagan message despite the fact that it was a commissioned painting on an established theme in Christian doctrine. Formally, he deviated from the delicate lyricism of his predecessors, such as his master Giovanni Bellini and his friend and rival Giorgione. The feminine figures in the painting emanate a vital sensuality, recalling the rules of classical antiquity, and the work as a whole presents great exuberance in its forms, colors, and textures. In this masterpiece from his youth, Titian already expressed the bombastic resourcefulness that would become his personal seal among the great artists of the Renaissance.

ate 1. *This Byzantine icon, a representation of the Mandylion, is painted not only*
a religious image but also as a sacred object that mediates between the artist and
energies of the celestial being it represents. The image is not intended to be a
turalistic reproduction of Christ but rather contains "errors" that correspond to an
borate deconstruction of forms that follows strict rules.

Plate 2. Sandro Botticelli's Primavera (1477–78) expresses a Hermetic description of the spiritual being's journey into the material reality of the manifest world. The different characters in this painting provide keys to the various parts of this journey, making coherent their inclusion in the scene.

Plate 3. In Piero di Cosimo's Death of Procris *(ca. 1500), the faun who places his hand on the dead nymph's left shoulder represents a savage and innocent being who existed in a time before Original Sin. The cloak covering Procris's hips is of an intense red, the triumphal color of alchemy.*

Plate 4. In The Garden of Earthly Delights *by Hieronymus Bosch (ca. 1504), the central panel—the source of the work's fame—shows a great number of peculiar scenes that mostly feature naked people. Although some of these characters' activities border on the obscene, the actions convey not a pleasant eroticism but rather an intentional asexuality. The artist wished not to praise corporeal beauty and sensual enjoyment but rather to expose the physical and spiritual misery of carnal sin.*

Plate 5. The Last Supper
by Leonardo da Vinci (1496–98)

*Plate 6. Does this depict a
woman among the apostles?
According to many exegetes, John
exhibits several typically feminine
features.*

Plate 7.

Plate 8. The Three Ages of the Woman and Death *by Hans Baldung (ca. 1510) is a allegory of the ephemeral.*

Plate 9. Melancholia I *by Albrecht Dürer (1514) illustrates the dangers and satisfactions of intellectual exploration and the contemplative life. Even the work's title confirms the symbolism. There was never a* Melancholia II; *this* I *is not a number, but the Latin word* i, *second person singular imperative of the verb* eo, *meaning "go." It is not only an allegorical engraving of melancholy but also a magical incantation for dispelling it from the artist's spirit.*

Plate 11. Self-Portrait
by Rembrandt (ca.
1660). The Flemish
painter executed
numerous portraits
of himself throughout
his life. This obsession
for capturing his own
face was not solely the
result of vanity—it
also stemmed from an
interest in studying
the traces of time and
experience on the
human face he knew
best.

Plate 10. Sacred and Profane Love *by Titian (1515–16). Each of the two feminine figures represent love. Divine love is represented by the nude Venus and profane love by the clothed Venus (the opposite of that which Catholic morality might lead us to understand). In mythology, nakedness symbolizes purity, innocence, and, above all, truth without pretense. Thus the painting shows the snares of profane and worldly love, emphasized by contrast with the absolute transparency of divine love.*

Plate 12. Belshazzar's Feast *by Rembrandt (Rembrandt Harmenszoon van Rijn) was created in 1635.*

Plate 13. The Ambassadors *by Hans Holbein the Younger (1533). The artist portrayed the diplomats Jean de Dinteville and Georges de Selve along with various objects that inform us of their identities. The future bishop is leaning his right arm on a book on the spine of which reads the Latin* Aetatis Suae 25, *meaning "his age is 25." This is the artist's homage to the prelate's young age. The ambassador's age, twenty-nine (29), is engraved on the hilt of his dagger.*

Plate 14. Saturn Devouring His Son *by Francisco de Goya (1821). A single character, a single terrified face, sufficed for the artist to convey the cruel mystery of life and death. Saturn was the Roman version of Chronos, the Greek god of time. Goya seems to be saying that we are all this son of Saturn; we will all be devoured by time, and meanwhile we consent to remain in chaos.*

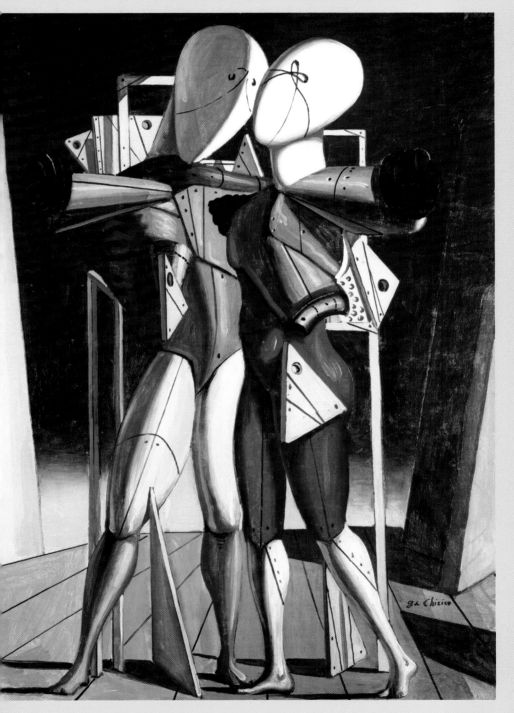

Plate 15. Hector and Andromache *by Giorgio de Chirico (1917). The figures are neither human nor mythological; they represent the helplessness and pain of existence. The advancing evening shadows are a clear metaphor for death.*

Plate 16. Perpignan Station *by Salvador Dalí (1965) is perhaps the most Hermetic and metaphysical work in the artist's entire pictorial development. Dalí considered this train station a magical place, a kind of world center pervaded by vibrations. For him, it was the axis of the mystery of the universe.*

Love in the Open Air

At the center of the scene in *Sacred and Profane Love* there is a large, open stone sarcophagus adorned with bas-reliefs and converted into a fountain. Leaning on this structure are two feminine figures with proud classical beauty, one richly clad and the other practically nude. Between them, an angelic Cupid dips a hand into the water in the pool. The young woman on the left, who looks at us from her seat on the edge of the sarcophagus, is wearing an expansive grayish-white garment with an ample neckline, above which flow her locks of fair hair. The figure on the right, who is looking at the other while leaning on the opposite end of the fountain, is covered only by a thin veil that hides her loins. On her left shoulder hangs a great, dark-red cloak that the wind (or she herself?) has drawn back so that the beauty of her nudity may be displayed.

The background is a landscape, far off but detailed, which appears to be inspired by the valleys of the northern Veneto, the artist's birthplace. To the left, on a mountainous outcropping, we can make out the rooftops of a village clustered around a tower or fortress. The panorama is interrupted at the center by a great mass of dark vegetation and continues at the right with a hunting scene that takes place in a meadow in which we can also see a flock of sheep and their shepherd. Behind this scene there is a lake, and farther back there is another town with a high church tower rising above it toward a cloudy evening sky. This twilight backdrop

The background of the painting is a landscape inspired by the valleys of the Veneto, the artist's place of birth.

contrasts with the bright carnality of the central figures, which Titian achieved with proximity and by contrasting a few basic colors that have been cleverly composed in a broad range of tones and shades.

Sacred Nakedness

Titian gave no title to his enigmatic work, or else it has been forgotten; *Sacred and Profane Love* is the result of later consensus. The Borghese Gallery, owner of this painting since the seventeenth century, made this the work's official name in 1833. Before then it had been known as *Unadorned Beauty and Adorned Beauty* (simply descriptive), *Three Loves* (synthetic and sloppy), and the more symbolic *Divine and Profane Woman*. The name the painting bears today and the recognition of the naked woman as the goddess Venus have come with the approval of authorized critics and scholars and are based not only on Titian's personality and other works but also on his membership in Neoplatonic circles and on the fact that the work was commissioned for the wedding of the Venetian aristocrat Niccolò Aurelio.

In accordance with the painting's accepted significance, the two female figures each represent love. The first surprise offered to us by exegetes who have studied this dichotomy is that divine love is represented by Venus, who is naked, while the clothed woman represents profane love. This is contrary to what Catholic morality may have taught, but Titian shared in the Renaissance ideas of the academy led by Marsilio Ficino and Pico della Mirandola, which returned to the pagan symbolism of classical Greece. In this mythology, nakedness signified purity, innocence, and, above all, truth without pretense (as in the expression "the naked truth"). Moreover, Titian suggests that the woman on the right came to the fountain covered by her great red cloak, then allowed or induced the wind to undress her in order to show her divinity in all its splendor. The woman on the left, on the other hand, exhibits a well-groomed elegance and wears jewels and a sumptuous garment with a suggestive neckline. Thus are shown the snares of profane and earthly love emphasized in contrast with the absolute transparency of divine love.

Hermetic Colors

Titian perfected and established the use of chromatism in painting, not only in the Renaissance, but also in subsequent centuries. This chromatic mastery coincided with his interest in the Hermetic meanings of colors and their values according to alchemy or astrology. *Sacred and Profane Love* is one of the first works in which this knowledge was applied, using a reduced chromatic scale whose symbolism is expressed by presence or omission. One example is the deep red of Sacred Love's cloak: It is the most sublime of the three Hermetic colors (the other two being black and white) because it symbolizes the completion of the Great Work of alchemy. In this work the goddess divests herself of this red, which is also the color of royalty and blood, and lets it flutter at her side before the remnants of a sky that is blue, another of the pure colors.

The use of the occult symbolism of color is also expressed through omission. In the personification of Profane Love there is no sign of the intensity we find in the great red cloak held up by the figure of Sacred Love. The initiated artist painted the clothed figure using a wide variety of colors—but all in attenuated, diffused shades. The shades used are as various as are the forms of profane love—maternal, filial, carnal, fraternal, and so forth—and the tone of each is softened because they represent earthly love, which is imperfect next to the purity of sacred love.

The Flame and the Rose

There are still more details offering keys to the painting's symbolism. The naked woman's arm is raised and holds an oil lamp whose flame represents spiritual and eternal love—that is, divine love. The clothed woman, by contrast, points with one finger to a wilted rose, symbolizing the ephemeral nature of profane love. This same arm is also curved around a chest, probably a jewel case, while the torso is inclined as if to protect it. This is an allusion to the egotism of earthly love as compared to the open and generous posture of divine love.

The artist also indicated this duality in the details of the painting's background. Behind Profane Love the landscape is abrupt and

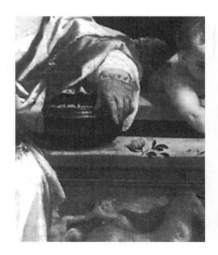

The flame of the oil lamp (left) symbolizes spiritual and eternal love. The finger pointing to the wilted rose (right) symbolizes the ephemeral nature of profane love.

culminates in a fortress, but the background of Sacred Love is a more serene landscape, with a church tower rising from it. In addition, the line of the horizon, divided into two distinct levels, makes the nude figure appear higher and more central, corresponding to her symbolism.

Finally, beyond the painting's magnificent and innovative technique, *Sacred and Profane Love* fulfills the ultimate goal that Renaissance esotericism required of great works of art: to preserve a mystery, a transcendent message, and to reveal it through colors, forms, individuals, landscapes, and details that can be interpreted to lead to sacred Hermetic knowledge. Titian handled the tools of this thaumaturgy with amazing skill.

HANS HOLBEIN THE YOUNGER
THE AMBASSADORS
(1533)

In this painting now in the National Gallery in London, a double portrait is filled with the artist's symbolic codes while a hidden yet very visible message recalls the inevitable presence of death. (See color plates 12–13.)

Death Mocks Human Vanity

When he painted these two young, upwardly mobile personalities of his epoch, Holbein included in *The Ambassadors* some symbols relating to his models. Such hidden details were common in sixteenth-century paintings and were flattering to patrons and commissioners, who enjoyed discovering them. In this work, however, the artist goes considerably beyond such innocent tricks, endowing the work with a symbolism that relates to the wisdom of his era in aspects that are both exoteric (visible and exposed) and esoteric (invisible and Hermetic).

The painting was executed on the occasion of a visit to London in April 1533 by the Frenchman Georges de Selve, elected bishop of Landau and plenipotentiary envoy of Francis I, and his meeting with his friend and countryman Jean de Dinteville, French ambassador to the English court. It was a delicate moment, for Henry VIII had just married Anne Boleyn without having the pope annul his previous marriage. The English monarch negotiated France's intervention before Pope Clement VII while he considered valid the divorce consecrated by the archbishop of Canterbury. This was the motive for Georges de Selve's voyage and, besides their mutual friendship, the reason for his meeting with the ambassador Jean de Dinteville. These minor historical characters probably would have been forgotten by now had they not posed for this famous work of art.

Discoveries and Schisms

History tends to call the sixteenth century the age of discovery thanks to significant advances in science and to oceanic voyages that revealed previously unknown routes and lands, thereby establishing once and for all the planet's spherical shape. Yet this progress of earthly knowledge corresponded to an era of crisis and confrontation in the spiritual realm.

In 1492 Columbus expanded the knowledge of lands by finding the New World, Elcano circumnavigated the globe in 1521, and Copernicus removed Earth from the center of the solar system in 1540. At this time, all kinds of knowledge advanced with a speed never before seen while established truths tottered and fell day by day. The Church was also in commotion, and the Vatican's avaricious abuses were shattering its prestige and its doctrine. With the support of the German princes, Martin Luther had initiated a Reformation that expanded over northern Europe, and in Geneva John Calvin exacerbated this schismatic rebellion. Adding to the deterioration of the authority of the Holy See, Henry VIII was preparing his own split from Rome, which he finalized in 1534 with the creation of the Anglican Church.

The Personal Symbols

Hans Holbein the Younger was no doubt well aware of all these affairs, and he reflected them symbolically in his painting. The two ambassadors he painted were politicians meeting to decide how to intervene in a religious crisis, and with their stern expressions and their neutral and impassive stares directed toward the viewer, the artist alludes to the diplomatic reserve they were obliged to maintain.

The sundial next to Jean de Dinteville's left hand indicates the date of this very important meeting is April 11, 1533. The future bishop is leaning his right arm on a book on the spine of which we can read the Latin words *Aetatis Suae 25,* meaning "his age is 25." This is the artist's homage to the prelate's young age. The ambassador's age, twenty-nine

(29), is carved in the hilt of his dagger. Also significant is the armillary sphere placed next to Jean de Dinteville, indicating his astronomical and geographical knowledge.

The Symbolic Objects

In the painting, Holbein separates the two subjects, which was not customary in double portraits of the time. Nevertheless, by separating them he centered the painting on a simple bookcase with two levels that contains a number of objects related to the science and culture of the Renaissance. On the upper shelf, which is covered by an Oriental rug, next to the aforementioned armillary sphere, we see various instruments intended for mathematical measurement and calculation. These symbolize the subjects'—and their epoch's—adherence to Pythagorean cosmogony.

The less cluttered lower shelf has on it a variety of objects. The most prominent of these is a large lute made of light-colored wood on which the light directly falls, perhaps to echo the white fur of the ambassador's coat on the opposite side of the painting. At the back of the shelf we can observe a small hand-globe, and at the front of the shelf we see a half-open book from which protrudes a square, another book of religious hymns lying open in front of the lute, and a few tubes for protecting plans or maps.

Experts often concur in their symbolic reading of these objects. The upper shelf reveals more or less that the universe is a mathematical creation (armillary sphere) which can be known and explained only through numerology (measuring instruments). The lower shelf reveals the sciences and arts of the Renaissance ruled by this mathematical absolute: geography, poetry, geometry, music, theology, and cartography.

There are two more interesting details in the painting: the lute, traditionally a symbol of harmony, has one broken string, symbolizing the rupture the Church has suffered. The open book on the shelf allows us to read part of a few hymns translated from Latin into German by Luther himself: "Come, Holy Spirit" and "The Ten

Commandments." Both of these express themes accepted by both Catholics and Protestants. It is possible that with these coded messages Holbein wished to honor the two ambassadors and their king, Francis I of France, whose ambition was to reunite the two Christian religions.

Death Lying in Wait

Less explicable is the large spindle-shaped object that appears to float above the floor in the lower third of the canvas, in obvious incongruence with the rest of the painting.

It is clear that this is not a real object in the sense that it does not form part of the room in which the ambassadors are posing. It must therefore come from another dimension, from another plane of the artist's creativity, and he must have put it there not on a whim, but with some cryptic meaning. Obviously, inclusion of this strange, prominent object went against the norms of portrait painting at that time and would have bothered anyone who wished to contemplate the work as a whole. Holbein must surely have had to gain the consent of his illustrious models to include it, and they would have had to accept the presence of this object and understand its occult significance.

This enigmatic thing, which had a definite influence in the fame of this work, is in fact an anamorphosis created using a technique

The distorted skull can be seen only when the painting is viewed from the right or left side and can be seen clearly only through a lens that modifies its proportions.

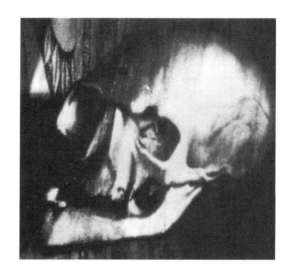

This is a re-creation of the distorted image.

invented by Leonardo da Vinci and explained in one of his notebooks. Holbein must have had access to this description and decided to use it in this painting to hide an esoteric symbol.

This element, in fact, comprises an extreme application of the laws of perspective, taking advantage of the optical illusion produced by the relationship between the angle of viewing of the object and the distance of the object observed. If we look at the painting straight on, as is customary, we see a shapeless and absurd element: the object without definition that seem to float above the floor. Yet if we step a few feet to the right and move closer to the wall on which the painting hangs, the object appears transformed into a skull.

Because the skull is the universal symbol for death, the occult message Holbein wished to transmit can be deciphered thus: Pride resulting from discoveries and scientific advances, vanity over works of art, desire for high offices, arrogance over vestments, and the fight over the doctrinal principles all become banal and absurd matters before the unavoidable end that awaits us.

REMBRANDT
BELSHAZZAR'S FEAST
(ca. 1635)

This magnificent painting by Rembrandt (Rembrandt Harmenszoon van Rijn), now hanging in the National Gallery in London, masterfully depicts the Bible story of the apparition of a strange message before the king of Babylon that only the Hebrew prophet Daniel was able to interpret. (See color plate 11.)

An Enigmatic Prophecy that Nobody Could Decipher
Belshazzar's Feast comes from Rembrandt's first period of painting in which he dedicated some of his works to depicting biblical themes. The expansion of Protestantism in the Dutch United Provinces had popularized the Hebrew scriptures, especially the passages referring to the castigation of vanity and luxury, sins feared by the prosperous Flemish bourgeoisie. Thus, both Christian and Jewish people gave abundant commissions for works of art depicting episodes drawn from the sacred book they shared.

The Ominous Message
The scene Rembrandt painted here was taken from the fifth chapter of the Book of Daniel, which must have been the work of many authors, considering the dubious existence of a patriarch with this name. The story takes place during the captivity of the Jews in Babylon. It tells how King Belshazzar, son and successor of the famous Nebuchadnezzar, holds a Dionysian banquet attended by thousands of nobles and their spouses and concubines. As part of the luxurious service, Belshazzar uses the offertory goblets and platters that his father stole from the temple of Jerusalem. In the moment depicted in the painting, a miraculous light emerges on one of the walls of the enclosure while a disembodied hand writes a message in Hebrew letters. The king summons his advisers and his Chaldean mages, but none of them can decipher this writing.

The biblical text relates: "Then was king Belshazzar greatly troubled, and his countenance was changed in him, and his lords were astonished." The queen then enters the hall, drawn by the commotion, and advises her husband to call upon Daniel the Jew, who has the ability to "interpret dreams, and shew hard sentences, and dissolve doubts." The disconcerted Belshazzar has the captive prophet brought forth, and Daniel translates the text, foretelling great misfortune for Belshazzar and his queen. The king dies that same night and Chaldea is soon conquered by King Darius of Persia.

A Biblical Snapshot

In this painting, as in *The Blinding of Samson* and *The Sacrifice of Abraham*, Rembrandt used imaginative resources to bring out the drama of the scene. The message and the mysterious hand writing it appear behind Belshazzar's back, so that he must turn his head to look at them while his body remains facing the table. This posture makes the scene look like a snapshot, freezing the king's expression of surprise, his profile lit by the mysterious light, while presenting a frontal view of the ostentatious luxury of his clothing and, in the foreground, Solomon's sacred vessels. The two figures on the left stare open-mouthed at the monarch's astonishment but not at the luminous message, which perhaps only he can see. The gesture of his left hand causes a corpulent lady at the right of the scene to bend in an exaggerated motion and spill the wine from her profaned chalice. Rembrandt painted in minute detail the jewels this woman wears in her hair as well as the pearls worn by the three figures on the far left. He also lavished detail on the king's crown, his ostentatious embroidered and jeweled cloak, his broaches, and his flashy bandolier of set gems. Undoubtedly, the artist gave priority to the signs of wealth that incited the divine wrath that brought the message.

Recent testing with advanced techniques has shown that the original painting was later manipulated. An anonymous hand slightly reduced the canvas on all four sides, causing the central characters to

The artist gave priority to ostentatious objects, such as the jewels worn by the figures in the painting, in order to emphasize the symbols of vanity and luxury.

stand out more. Another hand—or perhaps the same anonymous one that altered the size of the canvas—darkened the entire upper left section of the painting, obscuring the crowd of figures in the scene's background. Some of them were probably musicians, as suggested by the flutist faintly visible behind the feathers on the hat of the seated woman facing away from the viewer. This large, dark area contrasts sharply with the head of the only woman whose face can be seen. Her features resemble those of the woman in Rembrandt's later portraits of his fiancée, Saskia van Uylenburgh, whom he married the year following the creation of this painting.

The anonymous modification, which eliminated what we may guess to have been a large number of people in the background, gives prominence to characters who may originally have been part of an indistinct group, thereby converting a tumultuous feast into what looks almost like a private dinner. In its formal aspect, the painting thus becomes skewed toward the right hand side by the weight of the luminous message, Belshazzar's face, and the plump shoulders and bosom of the woman spilling her wine.

The Coded Writing

Artists who previously painted this biblical scene wrote the mysterious message in Latin, a language that was understandable to their educated contemporaries. Rembrandt decided to break this tradition, however, writing it in Hebrew letters. Yet this attempt at historical verisimilitude conflicted with the verse in the Book of Daniel (5:8): "Then came in all the king's wise men, but they could not read the writing, nor make known to the king the interpretation thereof." It would surely have been strange for the wise men of Babylon not to know Hebrew, considering the close contact between the Babylonians and the Hebrews during the time of captivity.

To resolve this contradiction, Rembrandt turned to Menasseh ben Israel, an erudite Jewish kabbalist who was also the artist's friend and neighbor. Menasseh suggested that the text must have been encoded in order to make it more difficult for the wise men and mages of the Babylonian court to decipher it. At his suggestion, a ciphered message was written in the painting. As we know, Hebrew text is read from right to left in the horizontal direction. The letters that appear in *Belshazzar's Feast* are arranged vertically and can be read column by column, likewise starting from the right.

Decoded according to this formula, the text reveals its enigmatic

A message in Hebrew letters foretells the misfortunes of King Belshazzar and his queen.

message: *mene, mene, tekel, ufarsin.* In the story, Daniel reads these words to Belshazzar after a lengthy speech about the king's father, the great Nebuchadnezzar, whose haughtiness led him to be dethroned and ridiculed. Daniel then reproaches the monarch, who still does not humble his heart, and the prophet then begins his famous diatribe against idolatry: "[T]hou hast praised the gods of silver, and gold, of brass, iron, wood, and stone, which see not, nor hear, nor know: and the God in whose hand thy breath is, and whose are all thy ways, hast thou not glorified."

With this warning stated, the exiled Jew explains to the king the content of the message. The literal meaning of the words it forms refers to the exploitation of minerals and to quantities of weight and measure. But Daniel—who, after all, was a prophet—interprets the words in the following manner (5:26):

> Mene, mene: God has counted your kingdom twice and put it to an end.
> Tekel: He has weighed you on his balance and your weight has not been sufficient.
> Ufarsin: Your kingdom will be divided and given up to the Medes and the Persians.

As mentioned earlier, the fearsome prophecy was fulfilled in an inexorable manner. Yet Daniel—whom Belshazzar, before dying, designated as one of the kingdom's viziers in gratitude for his service—went on to hold a prominent office under King Darius and his son, Cyrus the Great. From this office he dedicated himself to preaching the word of the God of Abraham, interpreting dreams, and delivering strange prophecies.

Glory and Misfortune

Rembrandt Harmenszoon van Rijn, who passed into history with only his first name, is recognized as the great master of the golden age of Flemish painting—the seventeenth century. *Belshazzar's Feast,* which he painted when he was about thirty years old, is one of his so-called baroque paintings, which are often undervalued by critics. This phase in the artist's career has recently been reevaluated, however, due to the painter's employment in these paintings of color, force, and movement—virtues that are attenuated in Rembrandt's later works, which are more serene and contemplative.

Throughout his life, Rembrandt painted himself in numerous self-portraits: oil paintings, engravings, and hasty sketches. (See color plate

10.) This obsession for capturing his own face was not solely the result of vanity—which he did not lack—but also stemmed from an interest in studying the traces of time and experience on the human features he knew best. Critics have pointed out that these studies served the artist as models for the people in his works—some of whom have a distinct similarity to the artist—or else were used for practicing and analyzing the expression of specific sentiments. Another use for self-portraits may have been to perfect the chiaroscuro technique.

Although he was lucky enough to enjoy fame as an artist during his lifetime—and gained, lost, then regained a considerable fortune—Rembrandt's private and family life was marked by bad luck. His beloved Saskia bore him four children between 1635 and 1641, but only one of these—Titus—survived. Saskia herself died in 1642. In 1649 the artist hired as his housekeeper a pretty young woman named Hendrickje Stoffels; she became his common-law wife and served as a model in many of his works.

The happiness of this second love and his pride in proportion to his fame as an artist and master led Rembrandt to squander the fortune he had gained from his art. In 1656 he declared bankruptcy, and in order to pay his debts, the valuable works he possessed—his own and those of others—were seized. He set to working feverishly to regain his estate, but the deaths of Hendrickje in 1663 and his son Titus five years later broke his remaining strength. He died on October 4, 1669. In subsequent years his work was practically forgotten until, a few decades later, his greatness began to appeal to the consideration of critics, the desire of collectors, and the funds of the great museums of the world. *Belshazzar's Feast* arrived in England in the eighteenth century after it was acquired by the Earl of Derby. It remained in the family mansion until 1964, when it was purchased by the National Gallery, where it can still be viewed today.

GOYA
SATURN DEVOURING HIS SON
(1821)

The great Spanish artist Francisco de Goya y Lucientes placed in his works messages and symbols that sought to express the dark dimension of existence, the anguish and terror of the passing of time, and unavoidable death. (See color plate 14.)

A Genius for Expressing the Otherworld

Goya's work includes numerous paintings and engravings depicting satanic and bacchanalian rituals attended by witches, demons, idols, fantastical beings, and monstrous, dreamlike figures. *Saturn Devouring His Son,* in Madrid's Prado Museum, is perhaps the synthesis and culmination of this entire otherworldly obsession: In it the artist required only a single character, a single terrified face, in order to convey the cruel mystery of life and death. This is not an illustration of a scene from classical mythology, but rather a medium for expressing on canvas existential desolation and terror.

A Tormented God

The choice of Saturn by an artist who was not very fond of depicting mythological characters is in itself thought-provoking. Saturn is the Roman version of Chronos, the Greek god of time, the incestuous offspring of Gaia (Earth) and her son Uranus, who engendered him in the pre-Olympian, atemporal chaos. According to myth, Saturn castrated and murdered his father in order to take his place, and the oracle sentenced him to be destroyed in turn by his own children. Therefore, Chronos-Saturn devoured them one after the other as they were born, and thus assumed consciousness and dominion over the passage of time. His wife, Rhea, managed to save one of the children, however, replacing him with a stone, which the god gulped down without realizing the trick. This saved son was Zeus, who overthrew Chronos and organized hierarchies and order on Olympus as well as in the terrestrial world that is its reflection. The worship of Chronos had great significance in Athens and Olympus, where he was represented as an old man brandishing a scythe for reaping grain because the agricultural cycle symbolized the wheel of life. The Romans perpetuated this worship and this image, giving him the name of Saturn—who is also known as the old man of the days in various pagan and esoteric creeds.

Goya portrayed Saturn at the crucial moment in his legend: when he is devouring one of his sons. He is portrayed without any stylization and with a kind of infuriated realism that gives the scene a disturbing degree of impact. The filicide occupies the central and upper part of the canvas, framed by the god's gigantic body, which fades away at the edges into the darkness of the background. Saturn does not bear the hard and implacable expression of a terrible god, but rather evinces abysmal anguish at his inhuman and inevitable action. His bulging eyes beg the nothingness for mercy, and his mouth appears to be forced to

Goya portrayed with an anguished realism the moment at which Saturn devours one of his children.

bite by the strong hands that grip the bleeding body of his son. The issue being eaten, with his back to us and already decapitated, is not a recently born child but an adult human being with a man's torso and feminine buttocks. The god's fingers, clenched around the child's waist, appear to separate these two halves. Goya seems to be telling us that we are this child of Saturn; we will all be devoured by time, and meanwhile we consent to remain in chaos.

The Feast of Chaos

Saturn Devouring His Son is not an isolated work; as was common for Goya, it formed part of a fairly coherent series. In this case, it is one of the group known as the Black Paintings, fourteen somber frescoes that the artist painted in the salon of the Quinta del sordo, the house he acquired in 1819. The master was already seventy-three years old at the time, and this estate near Manzanares was a refuge where he could free his creative imagination and give expression to the phantasms that pursued him.

Some authors connect the fresco *Saturn Devouring His Son* with the *Feast of St. Isidore*. In this painting, the title of the celebration, which originated in Madrid, masks a scene alluding to the feasts of the Roman Saturnalia. This Black Painting contains nothing festive and much that is gloomy and Dantean. It shows a group of contorted faces in a pyramidal position, some of them singing in chorus to the music of a guitarist in the foreground. Behind the guitarist stand cloaked figures wearing grayish robes with high lapels and hats pulled down tightly.

In ancient Rome, the feasts of Saturnalia, lasting from December 17 to 23, paid homage to Saturn as the god of the chaos that came before order. During these seven days, social dignities and differences were abolished, prohibitions were lifted, and everything was allowed. The authorities typically withdrew to their rural villas, and the people elected a carnivalesque king, usually a beggar or a servant of low standing. All order was subverted by the reign of parody and confusion.

Ladies acted like whores, whores were honored as matrons, patricians were forced to display their backsides, thieves dispensed justice, and magistrates were persecuted and beaten with rods. This chaos, highly amusing for its participants, expressed a secret nostalgia for the savage ancestral past, the true face of a world that, as the Cathars believed, had been created by Satan.

The Witches' Idol

Another infernal figure repeated in Goya's work is the goat, the mythological satyr and the idol Baphomet worshipped by secret medieval societies, including—according to the Inquisition—the Templars. In symbology, this goat is associated with the devil and the depiction of the ruthless father, with a secondary attribution as the bearer or messenger of evil.

This creature appears in the second of the *Scenes of Witches* painted in 1798 for the Alameda de Osuna. In the painting the beast is shown seated at the center, his great horns decorated with a wreath. Almost the entire front of his body can be seen except for the loins, which are hidden by the head of a witch who lies in the foreground with her back to us. The other witches are arranged in a circle around the deified beast. The one who appears to be the youngest offers the idol a plump baby, an older witch holds a very emaciated one, and a third baby lies on the ground, dying or dead. In the background we can see a pole from which hang infantile cadavers. We might think the series represents the stages in the extermination of a child, paraphrasing Saturn's anthropophagy that maintains his evil reign.

The goat appears again in another of the Black Paintings, *El Aquelarre* (The Witches' Sabbath). Here he is only a great dark silhouette with an unmistakable profile covered by what looks like a cloak or cape. Next to him is a figure with a distorted face, mutilated from the waist down and wearing a kind of white, monastic habit. The rest of the canvas is filled with witches who stare at the satanic idol with faces contorted by grimaces of astonishment, mistrust, and fear.

Scenes of Witches, *1798. At the center is the goat, an infernal figure repeated in other works by Goya.*

Capricious Nightmares

Goya painted *Los Caprichos* (The Caprices) between 1796 and 1798, shortly after the serious illness that left him deaf. The first part consists of humorous or gloomy scenes that caustically censure various evils of the time in a very personal style that came to be identified as Goyaesque. From the forty-third engraving to the eightieth and last, the artist switched registers. Using what he called "the credible monstrous," he created nightmarish scenes populated by witches, goblins, vampires, monks, demons, owls, and fantastical beings, among which occurs, once again, the figure of the goat.

This animal's presence as an evil symbol is apparent in three of these engravings. In number 56, whose title is *Subir y Bajar* (Rise and Fall), a giant with goat's feet (the anthropomorphic version of the goat) is shaking a few poor mortals in the air. In number 58, *Trágala Perro* (Swallow It, Dog), the central subject is a figure wielding an enormous syringe menacingly. As is usual with Goya, indistinct figures hover in the background. Among them we can discern the head of a goat with dark tape wrapped around its horns, recalling the infernal idol of Baphomet. Finally, in engraving number 60, *Ensayos* (Trials), an animal with a goat's head and a body more like that of a horse presides over a scene in which a young, naked woman appears to torture a man, who is also naked. In the foreground, two cats and a skull add mysterious symbolism to the engraving.

Los Caprichos were not well received by the Inquisition, which judged with mistrust Goya's irreverent mockery and the heresy enacted by his demons and witches. Warned that the Holy Office might order the destruction of the engravings, Goya presented them as a gift to his patron, King Charles IV.

A Cryptic Message

Some have claimed that Goya was a Freemason, which would not be surprising for a well-educated free spirit at the end of the eighteenth century. Yet no proof exists of his membership in this prestigious secret

According to one legend, Goya was buried without his head.

society, but there is proof of his anticlerical mysticism. His esoteric interests and his inclination toward the mysterious, the clandestine, and the macabre—together with his social rebellion—were in keeping with the more personal undercurrents found in his work. In his creations it is hard to miss the cryptic message, a mass of Hermetic symbols and codes infused by the breath of superhuman dimension.

The great artist, born in Fuendetodos, died in exile in Bordeaux in 1828 at eighty years of age. According to one legend, he was buried without his head.

GIORGIO DE CHIRICO
HECTOR AND ANDROMACHE
(1917)

This painting, now in the Galleria Nazionale d'Arte Moderna in Rome, is perhaps the most suggestive of the artist's obsessive and solitary quest to capture an image that would reach a metaphysical dimension entirely beyond visible reality. (See color plate 15.)

An Emblem of Metaphysical Art

This work, with its mythological title, is one of the most archetypal works of the period during which Giorgio de Chirico founded, christened, and led his personal movement of metaphysical art whose profound and Hermetic symbolism remains a subject of discussion among experts. In *Hector and Andromache* the two characters appear standing, stripped of all references to Homer's *Iliad*. As in other works by this artist, the figures look like anonymous dummies or mannequins dressed in absurd clothes and flanked by two reddish blocks that suggest strange buildings in a dreamlike scene that defies the rules of perspective. The heads have been replaced (or covered) by egg-shaped helmets that have empty dots for eyes from which droop thin lines to suggest abstract tears.

From shoulders to waist, the two characters' bodies exhibit a conglomeration of triangles and indeterminate polyhedral objects, while the legs are covered with tight-fitting stockings in medieval style. Behind the two rises a sort of frame made of thin boards, which appears to hold the mannequins upright. A powerful and hard light illuminates half of Hector's head, makes a dark terraced section that stretches out from the lower right corner of the painting, and causes the mannequins to cast long shadows. A yellow strip below the dark green background suggests a melancholy sunset that is just as unreal as the rest of the scene. To emphasize the metaphysical enigma of the work, Giorgio de Chirico avoided alluding to any place in space or moment in time.

Everything in the work is immobile, distant, and illusory and appeals to no sentiment other than its own mystery.

Hermetic Inspiration

This painting has been given various interpretations, starting with the artist's declared intention of "stripping art of what is common about it, what is accepted by the masses, and completely abolishing man as the guide and medium for expressing symbols." From this approach, the figures in *Hector and Andromache* are neither human nor mythological but instead signify the helplessness and pain of existence. The buildings represent the eternal indifference of matter, and the shadows lengthening with the sunset are a clear metaphor for death.

It has been pointed out that the dominant colors, green and red, are those used in Masonic ceremonies, that red is also the magical color of alchemists, and that the shadow advancing over the ground suggests a step pyramid from the pagan rituals of Babylon. Giorgio de Chirico, however, was born in Greece, where he lived until he was seventeen years old, and it is more likely that his metaphysics were inspired by the enigmatic Hermes Trismegistus and the texts of the *Corpus Hermeticum*. In a self-portrait from his old age, a statue of Hermes appears behind the artist, as if it was a protecting or inspiring figure.

Painting the Mystery

Giorgio de Chirico began his experiments in metaphysical painting in 1911, when he was only twenty-three years of age. Starting with suggestive models such as the empty plazas of Turin and Ferrara, he painted scenes in which volumes and spaces acquired an extracorporeal quality and human figures appeared distant, shapeless, and faceless. In 1915, while recovering in a military hospital in Ferrara, he met the futurist painter Carlo Carrà, who took an interest in his investigations.

Two years later, Giorgio joined forces with his younger brother, Andrea de Chirico, a painter, musician, and man of letters as talented and eccentric as the artist himself. Andrea went by the pseudonym Alberto

Savinio, and the two brothers attended meetings along with Carrà. They subsequently established metaphysical art, which was dedicated to expressing the nonrational dimension of existence. Giorgio adopted the practice of this ideology in the construction of magical and fantastical spaces in which were placed nonexistent objects and unreal people. In the same year, 1917, he painted two masterpieces in this deliberately mysterious style: *Hector and Andromache* and *The Great Metaphysician*. The latter depicts a tall, vertical contraption made of various metallic pieces in reddish shades and crowned by a typical de Chirican head (oval and faceless). The absurd and disturbing stateliness of this mechanical person contrasts with the serene perfection of the classical buildings rising in the background.

To evaluate Giorgio de Chirico's bizarre talent in its entire scope, we must remember that in that same year Apollinaire coined the term *surrealism,* a principally literary movement that spread to painting considerably later. Thus, Giorgio de Chirico cannot be considered as influenced by the surrealists, but rather as a solitary and exceptional precursor to them. This was the role he assumed upon arriving in Paris in 1924, when the poets André Breton and Louis Aragon began publishing *The Surrealist Revolution* as part of the movement that aspired to shake the foundations of artistic creation. Giorgio de Chirico was received by them with enthusiasm; he participated in various issues of the magazine and in the first exhibition at the Pierre Gallery in 1925.

Shortly afterward, however, the metaphysical artist began feeling uncomfortable in the exclusive group of the surrealists, especially because of their insistence on the dreamlike and their "revolutionary" rebellion, which Giorgio de Chirico considered frivolous and superficial. In 1926, Breton accused him of "substituting the inspiration of dreams with the artificial respiration of painting," which annoyed the painter, who subsequently described the surrealists as "foolish and hostile."

From this time on, he separated from the group, although his work exercised a strong influence over René Magritte, Max Ernst, Salvador Dalí, and other great artists within the surrealist movement.

An Obsessive Theme

Giorgio de Chirico had more than fifty years of creative activity, during which time he developed a body of work that was always original and his own and that exhibited a complete lack of interest in the artistic fads and currents going on around him during his long lifetime. After his separation from the surrealists, he abandoned the formal aspects of his metaphysical period, but his work continued to emanate enigmatic mystery, frequently expressed by a highly personal treatment of the rules of classicism. In a certain way, his art continued to be Hermetic in nostalgic homage to the memories and readings of his adolescence in Athens.

In sketches and outlines as well as in completed works, Giorgio de Chirico returned several times to depicting the Homeric couple Hector and Andromache. Notable among these are the 1926 bronze sculpture in which the faces are again hidden beneath masks and the canvas with the same title painted in 1974. In this work, the two characters exhibit human anatomy and are depicted in a classical landscape, but the author still refrained from showing their facial features. Hector is again covered by his neutral oval helmet, this time adorned with a plume of feathers, giving him a certain Hellenic air. Andromache, naked with long red hair, embraces him with her back to the viewer, who once again cannot see her face.

Some critics have attributed this reiteration of the Homeric theme to pacifist symbolism because it portrays the moment when the hero and his beloved bid farewell to each other before he departs for the Trojan War. Although this interpretation should not be entirely ignored, Giorgio de Chirico's obsession with Hector and Andromache appears to reflect a message that is more transcendent and at the same time more obscure. The scene does not occur in Troy, nor amid World War I, which was ravaging Europe at the time of the first painting, but in a space without geography and a time existing in another dimension. It expresses a metaphysical enigma, which, like its symbolic figures, refuses to show its face.

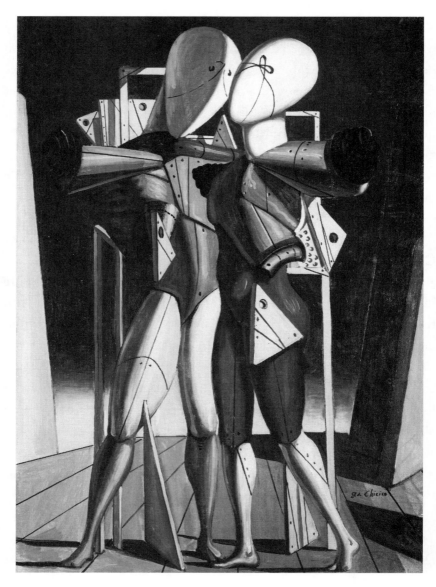

De Chirico decontextualized his figures geographically and did not show their faces.

SALVADOR DALÍ
PERPIGNAN STATION
(1965)

In this work, Salvador Dalí combined cryptic elements from a painting by Millet with the dreamlike intuitions of his paranoiac-critical method in order to create a vision of the center of the universe. (See color plate 16.)

The Most Mysterious Work in the Genre of Surrealism

Dalí himself pointed out that *Perpignan Station* (now in the Ludwig Museum in Köln, Germany) was the most Hermetic and metaphysical work in all of his prolific artistic production. "It is always in Perpignan Station that the most brilliant ideas occur to me," he claims in his autobiography, *Mi vida secreta* (My Secret Life). "There I see the fourth dimension," he adds, "through the overlapping of parabolic lenses, as in a fly's eye." The artist considered the train station to be a magical place, a kind of world center pervaded by vibrations: the axis of the mystery of the universe, like Pascal's sphere or the Aleph, defined by Borges as "the place where all the places of the world are, seen from all angles."

Salvador Dalí finished this painting when he was sixty-one years old, at the height of his popularity, which was due both to his genius and his eccentricity. He had always shown an enthusiastic admiration for scientific advances; his idols in this field were Albert Einstein and Sigmund Freud, who were both great influences on his work. Although his inspiration from psychoanalysis and the world of dreams is very obvious, he was also interested in antimatter and quantum physics and was fascinated with the discovery of the genetic chain of DNA.

The Lines of the Universe

In *Perpignan Station* there are four distinct lines of force leading outward from the exact center of the painting and expanding toward the four corners, like intense solar rays. Dalí once called them "the lines of the universe," without offering further explanation. At the central vertex, where the rays unite, the figure of a man is suspended in the air with his legs and arms extended outward, as if he is immobilized in the middle of a leap. A larger version of this figure is repeated higher up on the canvas. Between the two men, who are one and the same, floats a strange, typically Dalían piece of furniture. In the lower part of the work, along the same vertical line, there appears a feminine image with her back turned to us. She seems to emerge from a framelike object that might be an enigmatic gadget or a Hermetic symbol.

At each side in the painting there stands a dark figure in the foreground: On the left is a man with his hat in his hand and on the right is a woman with her hands joined and a farmer's pitchfork. In the background on the left side, indistinct in the fog, there are two silhouettes and a sack and wheelbarrow. On the other side, also in the background, two misty figures comprise a woman bent over and a man who seems about to copulate with her. Because all of the people in the painting are depicted against the light or shrouded in fog, as is often the case in Dalí's works, we cannot see their faces.

The esoteric interpretation of *Perpignan Station* begins with the single element that Dalí defined: the yellow rays that dominate the painting, representing the lines of the universe. The man is thus at its center but is also duplicated in space. This space, which also serves as a background, is a cosmos without gravity, a nebulous indefinite in which float other symbolic figures. The man and woman occupying the far sides of the work might be understood as the essential, primordial, Edenic man and woman. The characters with the wheelbarrow symbolize work, and the copulation scene represents sexuality. Dalí's chests always represent memory, and the floating piece of furniture in the upper center of the work has been interpreted as containing the universal memory of humanity. The presence of the painter's other obsession—death—is less evident. Perhaps it can be found in the small woman with her back turned who stares immobile at the cosmic man.

In this painting, Dalí portrayed his metaphysical vision of the essence of the world as it converged upon the Perpignan railway sta-

Perpignan Station, *a metaphysical vision of the Dalían world*

tion. For him, this vision also originated from his passion for the most recent scientific discoveries of the time: the theory of multiple universes, the relativity of time and space, and the Freudian subconscious. The majority of experts view the man duplicated along the vertical axis of the painting as an allusion to antimatter. Some bolder interpretations, however, have suggested that this figure might be a brilliant prediction of cloning, a genetic marvel based on the manipulation of DNA.

If the painting had no title, viewers would not have known that its subject was the Perpignan train station. Dalí included no reference to this location, not even an allusive one; his interest lay in painting the Aleph hidden within himself, the magic nucleus reflecting all the dimensions and moments of the universe.

The Metaphysical Master

If, in *Perpignan Station,* Dalí unleashed his magnificent esoteric intuitions and his passion for advances toward the limits of science, a third and fundamental reading leads us to his interest in the metaphysics of art. Dalí, the arrogant genius from Port Lligat who publicly denounced all the artists of his time, had an absolute veneration for a little-known nineteenth-century French painter, Jean-François Millet. During his stay in Paris in 1933, Dalí became fascinated with Millet's work *The Angelus,* painted in 1859. The piece shows a peasant couple who have interrupted their work for evening prayer.

According to Dalí, Millet concealed a message of transcendent Hermeticism in this simple rural scene, revealing gifts of perception at least as great as Dalí's own. In the same year, Dalí reproduced the canvas in the upper corner of his painting *The Angelus of Millet Preceding the Imminent Arrival of the Conical Anamorphosis,* a title which—besides being an homage to his recently discovered mystical forerunner—reflects Dalí's exploration of pictorial techniques with the purpose of concealing mysterious symbols, as in the anamorphosis invented by Leonardo da Vinci (see pages 68–69 in the commentary on Holbein's *The Ambassadors*). Also in this same year, the Catalan artist wrote a text entitled *The Tragic Mystery of Millet's* The Angelus, in which he credits Millet with the inspiration for the paranoiac-critical method that was Dalí's personal approach to surrealist thinking.

More than thirty years later, in 1964, Salvador Dalí employed his old friend Ricardo Sánchez, who had been one of the technicians for the film *El pierro andaluz,* to pose as a male model for *Perpignan Station,* while the ever-present Gala (Salvador's wife) served as a female model. The painting is, among many other things, an obvious homage to Millet. Essential elements from *The Angelus* appear in it, though instead of being simply transferred from the original painting, they are redistributed in the esoteric plane of the Dalían canvas. The two peasants are copied almost exactly from those in Millet's piece, but they are separated and placed on opposite sides of the painting. The pitchfork that the French painter depicted stuck vertically into the ground next to the man appears leaning in front of the woman in Dalí's work. The wheelbarrow with sacks of grain can be seen in the misty background,

Photograph of the eccentric mage of surrealism, Salvador Dalí

along with the two silhouettes carrying or laying down their sacks. The figures Dalí added in the background appear as holographs or clones of the peasant couple: It is these two who toil with the wheelbarrow and who seem about to commit a sexual act. (In this scene in the painting the woman is bending over to touch the ground with what appears to be a sack of hay.)

All these figures taken from *The Angelus* give a new meaning and framework to Dalí's exclusive contribution: the enigmatic central vertical axis and the diagonal rays. Various critics have observed that what gives *Perpignan Station* its mysterious transmutation is not the elements reproduced from *The Angelus* or Dalí's fantastic ideation, but rather the unique and almost magical relationship among all the components of the painting. It seems as if the great surrealist painter succeeded in calling up the spirit of his esoteric master so that the two of them might create one of the most suggestive and cryptic works of universal art.

SCULPTURE

The principal characteristic of sculpture is its embracing of the three physical dimensions, along with the durability of its materials, such as stone, marble, and metals. These qualities make it the optimal art for creating monuments and statues of a mythical or religious character, and in one way or another, it has been present in nearly all known civilizations.

In the West, the first sculptures appeared in ancient Egypt and soon afterward in the Mediterranean civilizations of Chaldea, Assyria, and Babylon. The imposing solidity of sculpture makes it very appropriate for representing gods in statues or as bas-reliefs in temples and plazas. The mystical and magical character of such sculptural works was often invoked in pagan ceremonies. Classical Greek art and, later, Roman art elevated sculpture to artistic and anatomical perfection, with statuary that honored figures and scenes from mythology as well as worldly figures (emperors, warriors, politicians, etc.).

Despite the fact that sculpture is an art that, due to its materials and techniques, requires concrete representations of reality, many sculptures have received various esoteric interpretations and references or have concealed mysteries regarding their true origin and meaning. Such is the case for the examples that are offered here.

ANCIENT EGYPTIAN ART
THE SPHINX OF GIZA
(ca. 2500 BCE)

The true age of this enigmatic monument in the Valley of Giza in Egypt, like its origin and the intent of its makers, has given rise to controversies and theories involving the Universal Deluge, Atlantis, and even possible extraterrestrial influences. (See color plate 17.)

An Antediluvian Monument?

Corroded and damaged, this monumental statue continues imposing its enigmatic presence over the Valley of Giza, near the Cairo suburbs. According to academic archaeology, it was constructed a little over four millennia ago, during the Fourth Dynasty, which began around 2500 BCE. According to this official story, its erection was an homage to the famous pharaoh Khafra, whose features are reproduced in the weathered face of the Sphinx. Yet these claims have been questioned in recent decades by dissident investigators who hail from other fields of knowledge. Some of them claim that the imposing Sphinx is about ten thousand years old and therefore predates not only the reign of Khafra but also the entire Egyptian civilization.

The enormous statue is located near the famous three pyramids and in front of one of the funerary temples in the sandy archaeological field of Giza. The Sphinx measures approximately 230 feet long by 66 feet tall. It was carved in this place from a natural limestone promontory and has never been moved. Originally, its perimeter was surrounded by a deep moat, probably to isolate the huge stone figure and give it a rectangular base. It represents an anthropomorphic animal with a lion's body, its front paws extended, and a human head covered by a pharaonic headdress. Sandstorms and floods have eroded the head considerably and the rectangular beard has broken off from the chin. This piece was later discovered in two fragments, which are kept at two museums, one in Cairo and one in London.

In the Age of Atlantis

The first questioning of the age and significance of the Sphinx was initiated by a singular personality. The mathematician and mystic R. A. Schwaller de Lubicz, who was French, developed a Hermetic code using the dimensions of various constructions from pharaonic architecture along with the measurements of statues, reliefs, and other Egyptian works of art. De Lubicz, who used the esoteric pseudonym *Aor,* applied his code to the Sphinx in 1952 and announced publicly that the statue and its base had been eroded by the waters of the Universal Deluge.

Scientific circles did not take seriously de Lubicz's claim, but a few years later it was repeated by another curious character, John Anthony West, a writer and an enthusiast of occultism who made his living authoring tourist guides on the Valley of Giza and other archaeological sites. West took advantage of his professional travels to nurture his great enthusiasm for the mysteries of ancient Egypt. An admirer of de Lubicz's work, in 1970 he released a series of theories inspired by the Sphinx. West claimed that if the monument had been constructed before the Deluge, then it offered irrefutable proof of the existence

R. A. Schwaller de Lubicz was known for developing a Hermetic code using the measurements and proportions of certain pharaonic monuments.

of Atlantis, the oceanic civilization submerged beneath the waters.

This claim was based on information that various defenders of this theory claimed to be true: Some survivors of the disaster must have entered the Mediterranean and landed in the Nile Valley. All this must have occurred nine or ten millennia ago as the consequence of a massive and devastating inundation.

These ideas aroused more or less serious interest in heterodox circles until West put some icing on the cake that made it harder to swallow: He contended that the Sphinx's features were the exact image of the "face" formed by a group of hills on the surface of Mars. Thus, he concluded, the Atlanteans must have formed the Sphinx with the guidance and collaboration of extraterrestrial beings. Discounting any alien presence, it is obvious that Egyptian astronomers did not have telescopes capable of making out the face on Mars—and neither did their hypothetical predecessors ten thousand years ago.

When It Rains, It Pours

The theories of de Lubicz and West were there for anyone who wanted to believe them, and they enjoyed consideration in certain mysterious

John Anthony West developed several esoteric theories regarding the Sphinx. According to him, its features are similar to the famous face formed by a group of hills on the surface of Mars.

After lengthy investigations, the geologist Robert Schoch concluded that the erosion on the Sphinx and its base is the result of rain, which called into question its age established by archaeologists.

circles. In 1991, however, a real scientist came on the scene and was ready to discuss the canonical story of the Sphinx: Robert Schoch was not an archaeologist but a geologist and researcher at Boston University. Schoch was working on new methods of using carbon for the advanced measurement of the age of mineral formations. In order to prove his method at this time, he needed a monument that was thousands of years old and whose age was already established with a strong degree of certainty. What better monument would serve this purpose than the great Sphinx of Giza, dated by archaeologists to the year 2500 BCE?

The eager geologist brought his instruments to Egypt to study the Sphinx. He established that the erosion on the monument and its base had been caused by heavy and continuous rain, which called into question the "exact" age established by archaeology. In the middle of the third millennium BCE, Egypt had a semiarid climate in which precipitation was unusual and light—not sufficient to erode any kind of stone. The climate had been this way for several millennia, with the last damp and rainy era occurring around 7000 BCE or earlier. Curiously, the pyramids and the other monuments of Giza were proved to date from the third millennium BCE. Thus Schoch concluded that the Sphinx must be older than the pharaohs' civilization, and thus could not have been erected as an homage to Khafra.

The Case of the Stone Faces

Official archaeologists do not recognize the Sphinx's great antiquity, although they accept that perhaps its face does not represent that of the pharaoh Khafra. On this subject another investigator had unexpected influence—this time, not a scientist but a policeman, Detective Frank Domingo of the New York Police Department. This expert's job was to draw the possible face of a suspect from the statements of witnesses or other pertinent information. To create this image, technically known as an Identi-kit, Domingo had been using a sophisticated computer program, which he had also helped to develop. Learning of the interdisciplinary controversy over the Sphinx and Pharaoh Khafra, he decided to take a vacation in Egypt to test the powers of his device.

Thus began what we might call, paraphrasing Erle Stanley Gardner's titles, the Case of the Stone Faces. Domingo took the anthropometric measurements of a statue of Khafra at the archaeological museum in Cairo, then compared them with the Sphinx's facial features. The differences were so obvious that neither erosion nor possible stylization could justify them. This seemed to confirm that whatever its age might be, the mysterious monument did not represent the famous pharaoh.

On the other hand, Robert Schoch himself had already noted

According to some scholars, the mysterious monument was not erected as an homage to Pharaoh Khafra.

that the Sphinx's head was very small in relation to its leonine body. Some conservative Egyptologists seized on this observation in order to maintain the theory that it was a sculpture of Khafra: The head was not in proportion to the body because the original had been replaced in 2500 BCE by the head and royal headdress of this pharaoh. This hair-splitting allowed them to concede one or two more millennia and accept that the rest of the Sphinx might be an earlier construction.

All these theories and hypotheses—none of which is completely provable—have only increased the mystery surrounding the Sphinx. Some authors have also connected the monument to astrology, the movements of the earth's axis, and celestial constellations. Meanwhile, like a vain elderly lady, the Sphinx carefully hides her age and prefers not to show her face.

THE HELLENISTIC SCHOOL
VENUS DE MILO
(SECOND CENTURY BCE)

The loss of its arms, both a fault and an enhancement of the absolute perfection of the *Venus de Milo,* is a mystery connected to ancient legends and modern political affairs. (See color plate 18.)

The Mystery of the Lost Arms

This extremely famous statue of the goddess Venus, now housed at the Louvre in Paris, was discovered accidentally in the early nineteenth century. Since then, it has been seen as an unparalleled model of feminine beauty, transcending the fashions, trends, and tastes of every era. Even considering that classical statuary defined an aesthetic that still survives today, the *Venus de Milo* has a mysterious appeal that goes beyond mere anatomical perfection.

Some have said that the secret of this strange magnetism resides in the statue's lack of arms, which bestows preeminence to the magnificently modeled torso and abdomen. This absence of the most expressive extremities of human anatomy has given rise to another mystery: Were the arms broken off from the body, or were they never there in the first place? Academic scholars are inclined toward the first option, although there is no shortage of arguments in favor of the second. There are also claims that the statue appears to be mentioned in historical and ecclesiastical documents that report pontifical prohibitions based on its exhibition and indicating that it is older than generally believed.

A Mortal Embrace

An ancient tradition circulating around the islands of the Aegean Sea attributes the lack of arms of the *Venus de Milo* to a passionate tragedy. According to this story, the most famous sculptor in the Peloponnese heard tell that on the island of Milos there lived a young lady of dazzling beauty. He went there, fell hopelessly in love with the young woman upon seeing her, and asked her to pose as a model for a statue of Venus. She accepted, and they shut themselves up in a cabin that served as the artist's studio.

The moment came when the statue was almost complete save the arms. (Versions of the story differ: Some say the arms had not even been begun; others say that all that remained to be done was to polish them and set them in place.) Come nightfall, the sculptor abandoned his work and invited his model to bed with him. She passionately threw herself upon him, offering him one of her shapely breasts. He took her nipple between his lips, and she, in the ardor of the embrace, gripped him so tightly that she prevented him from breathing. The poor man could not escape and died of asphyxiation. Thus the *Venus de Milo* ended up without arms—and those who tell the story say that few deaths have ever been so beautiful.

The only documentary support for this story is an ancient Armenian text that tells of a statue called the *Drowned Man's Venus,* but it is not clear whether it refers to the same sculpture. It is also said that in the eighth century the Vatican prohibited the exhibition of a marble nude disparagingly referred to as *The Armless.*

The Adventures of the Most Beautiful Goddess

The *Venus* was found in 1820 on the island of Milos (also known as Milo or Melos) in the Aegean Sea. Its discoverer was a farmer named Yorgos, who disinterred it, broken in two halves and with the hair detached from the head. He confided the discovery to his confessor, a monk named Oconomus, who offered Yorgos seven hundred fifty piasters for the statue. Yorgos's family clan considered the offer insufficient, however, and tried to sell it to Dumont d'Urville, an officer aboard a French ship anchored in the port who had shown a lively interest in the statue. The farmer asked him for twelve hundred piasters, but the young mariner did not have this much money and had to give up the purchase. Surely, it was he who brought the news to Constantinople, to the secretary of the French embassy, a young diplomat by the name of Marcellus. The secretary suggested persuading the ambassador, the marquis of Rivière, to purchase the *Venus*.

Marcellus and d'Urville convinced the Navy lieutenant Materer, commander of the frigate *Estafette,* to transport them to Milos with the intent of taking possession of the *Venus*. Upon arriving at the port of the island, however, they met some Turkish soldiers who were packing up the pieces of the statue to take it away. At the time, Milos belonged to the Ottoman Empire and the imperial government assumed rights over anything that was found there. The intruders attacked and a bloody battle followed in which the statue changed hands several times, ultimately being seized by the French.

Ambassador Rivière gave thanks for the gift in the face of protestations from the Ottoman government and the authorities of the island, not to mention vengeful threats from Yorgos's clan. The marquis was an astute diplomat and, with great finesse, made reparations for the injury. He offered excuses to the Turks, telling them the local governors of Milos were responsible; he apologized to the local governors, blaming the oppressive Empire; and he appeased the anger of Yorgos and his relatives with a gift of six thousand francs, which he charged to the embassy's accounts. He did all this—but he certainly did not return the statue. In order to end up on top of the situation and to avoid further problems, he immediately sent the carving to France as

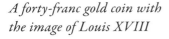

A forty-franc gold coin with the image of Louis XVIII

a personal gift to King Louis XVIII. The monarch passed it on to the Louvre Museum. There the pieces were reunited, and the statue was set up in the special room where it is still exhibited today.

The Arms of Venus

The romantic and beautiful fable of the sculptor and his homicidal model is actually as false as the claim that the *Venus de Milo* was found without arms. It appears that this last story was invented by Ambassador Rivière as an excuse for giving the king a damaged work of art. In fact, during the battle at the port of Milos, the pieces of the statue apparently fell on the stone of the breakwater, causing the arms to break from the body. Since then, these pieces of marble, surely as beautiful as the rest of the statue, have remained at the center of a mysterious controversy.

Another version claims that Yorgos had also found the left hand, holding an apple, attached to part of the forearm and that he succeeded in hiding this piece when the Turkish imperial soldiers came. It is said that the hiding place was passed on from generation to generation by the chiefs of the island's three families, descendants of Yorgos's clan.

In the 1960s, a commission of Turkish archaeologists presented a petition to the French minister of culture, André Malraux, in which they reclaimed ownership of the *Venus de Milo*. This claim was based on a complete report by the jurist Ahmed Rechim. Along with documenting the fact that in 1820 the island of Milos belonged to the Ottoman Empire, the report accused Marcellus and his accomplices of having literally stolen the statue and accused Rivière and Louis XVIII of having accepted it while being aware of its criminal origin. Rechim added that the statue was an ancient part of Turkish artistic heritage, that it had been buried on the remote island of Milos to protect it from robbing and pillaging, and that Yorgos's discovery was an unfortunate accident. The report affirmed the existence of the arms and stated that only three families knew their hiding place. Rechim concluded with an offer: If France returned the statue, Turkey would put the arms back

*André Malraux, French
minister of culture during the
1960s, flatly refused to return
the* Venus de Milo *to Turkey.*

in place and give to the world this great artistic masterpiece in all its original splendor. If, however, France did not return it, the *Venus de Milo* would continue displaying its stumps in the Louvre Museum.

Malraux responded that such a proposal was cultural blackmail and flatly refused to return the statue, declaring: "The *Venus de Milo* is as French as La Marianne" (the idealized Phrygian cap–wearing revolutionary who is the emblem of the republic of Gaul). The Turkish government chose not to enter into debate with proud and *grandeuse* France, which was presided over by Charles de Gaulle. In a press memo, it explained that this affair had been an honorable private initiative on the part of Rechim and the archaeologists, but that it was absolutely not official in nature.

Since then, art historians have continued asking the great question: Is it true that the Turkish government and the farming people of Milos know the hiding place of the lost arms—or was the suggestion of their hiding place a ruse developed by Rechim and based on groundless legends in order to pressure Malraux?

IBERIAN ART
LADY OF ELCHE
(FOURTH CENTURY BCE)

This small and famous Iberian sculpture now housed in the National Archaeological Museum in Madrid presents unsolved enigmas as to its identity and origin and gives rise to controversy regarding its clothing and decoration. (See plate 19.)

A Mysterious and Ambiguous Woman

On the morning of August 4, 1897, the laborers at an estate near Elche, or Elx, in Alicante, Valencia, stopped work to eat lunch. The youngest of them, a lad by the name of Manolico, continued working on the slope of a hill that was known as La Alcudia. In the days of the Iberians, a river had wound around this promontory not far from the town of Helike. The Romans had Latinized this name, calling their settlement at this spot Illici Augusta Colonia Julia. Finally, the Arabs converted it into Elche, a name that endured through the ensuing centuries.

As he worked, Manolico's hoe struck against something solid. Together, he and his companions cleared away a few stones that covered a hollow in the earth. The youth carefully removed a stone bust of remarkable beauty. This accidental archaeological discovery caused a sensation and was the starting point for the consolidation and expansion of investigations into Iberian culture. According to custom, archaeological pieces are named after the places where they have been discovered, and so this bust became famous as the *Lady of Elche*. Manolico and the people from his area, however, continued to refer to it by the name they had given it: *The Dead Queen*.

A Well-Dressed Lady

It is likely enough that the *Lady of Elche* was originally a complete statue that perhaps took a seated position. This assumption is based on the fact that the bust has no base and its underside is irregular, as if it had been broken off. Even with only the upper part, however, we can appreciate a magnificent work of art that is on par with the best of its era and is fascinating in its perfect workmanship and its aura of mystery. It is a relatively small piece (about 22 inches tall), which makes all the more remarkable the meticulous chiseling of its clothing, jewelry, and headdress, which must have been arduous.

The first aspect of its appearance that draws attention is the pair of large disc-shaped coils that completely cover the two sides of its head. This hairstyle can be seen on other such statues of women excavated at Iberian sites, and it impressed the Greek cartographer Artemidorus when he visited this area in the year 100 BCE. The discs are supported on their surfaces by radial pieces, and their edges are decorated with small spheres, perhaps pearls, which also form a diadem with three lines over a tight-fitting hairnet that covers the entire head.

The clothing worn by the *Lady of Elche* consists of three articles: a thin interior tunic that shows above the neckline of a dress; a covering dress of which only the front can be seen; and over this, a half-open cape with lapels that hang over the back of the neck. The anonymous artist's real tour de force, however, is in the elaborate ornaments rendered in admirable detail. One curious fact is that the sculptural display on the front of the statue does not correspond to the back of the piece, which exhibits only a sizable and enigmatic hole.

The Impenetrable Face

As a contrast to the ostentatious clothing and elaborate jewelry that decorate the *Lady of Elche,* her face expresses an austere serenity that appears to go beyond her showy attire. Some have pointed out that her expression is similar to that of the *kouroi* or votive statues in ancient Greek art. The straight nose, which continues from the forehead without any pronounced bridge, appears to confirm this hypothesis. Some remainders of paint can be seen in the well-defined mouth, and the lips, pressed together lightly, show just the hint of an ambiguous smile at the left corner of the mouth.

The air of mystery and power conveyed by the statue's contemplation resides essentially in the eyes. Usually, Iberian sculptures have round eyes that are fairly inexpressive, but the *Lady of Elche* has elongated eyes that are almost Asian, with eyelids that are closed halfway over pupils consisting of small hollows which at one time likely contained beads or jewels set in the stone, to give brilliance to the statue's stare. The effect is that the woman appears to look at the viewer with aristocratic loftiness while, at the same time, she looks within herself into a dimension impenetrable to us.

Dama del Cerro de los Santos, *an Iberian stone sculpture (ca. fourth century BCE or later): This sculpture of an Iberian woman has some similarities to the* Lady of Elche.

Plate 17. Sphinx of Giza (ca. 2500 BCE). This monumental and enigmatic sculpture presents an anthropomorphic animal with a lion's body, the front paws extended, and a man's head covered by a pharaonic headdress. According to the official story, it was built as an homage to the famous pharaoh Khafra, whose features are reproduced in its weathered face.

Plate 18. Venus de Milo, *the essence of feminine beauty (second century BCE). The question of whether the arms were broken off or whether they were never sculpted is still debated.*

Plate 19. Lady of Elche (fourth century BCE). The enigma of this anonymous bust resides in its disputed gender identity as well as in the large hole in the back of the sculpture.

Plate 20. David *by Michelangelo Buonarroti (1501–4). Traditionally, David is depicted next to the head of the slaughtered Goliath, but the marble block available t[...] Michelangelo was too small for this depiction. The artist surmounted the difficulty b[...] sculpting the valiant shepherd at the moment of entering into combat with the giant.*

Plate 21. Perseus with the Head of Medusa *by Benvenuto Cellini (1554). Perseus was ...le to take Medusa by surprise, and, looking in his mirrorlike shield in order to avoid ...ing turned to stone, he decapitated her with a single blow from the sword of Hermes.*

Plate 22. *The Great Pyramid of Cheops (ca. 2570 BCE), designed by the architect Hemon. The priests and astrologers of pagan cults believed that the shape of the pyramid possessed enigmatic powers. It is not understood how the ancient Egyptians managed to transport the stone from more than six hundred miles away without the use of wheels or how they cut the stone into blocks, raised the blocks more than three hundred feet, and placed them in precise position without the use of cranes or pulleys. Above all, it is not known how the Egyptians situated the Great Pyramid and the other two pyramids in the Valley of Giza at the same proportional distances and angles found among the three main stars in the constellation Orion.*

Plate 23. Chartres Cathedral (twelfth–thirteenth centuries). Hermetic tradition relates that in Jerusalem the Templars discovered the Ark of the Covenant buried beneath the stables of the Temple of Solomon and that the order's mission was to protect it and prevent it from falling into profane hands. The Templars, the secret builders of Chartres Cathedral, may have hidden the Ark between the church's walls, in a place where only they could access it by means of an initiatory portal.

Plate 24. Notre Dame in Paris stands on an island in the midst of the city, flanked by two channels of the Seine. To reach the island and cathedral a pilgrim must "cross the waters," an essential initiatory act in many ancient cults.

Plate 25. The rose window in Notre Dame Cathedral, Paris, like all rose and stained-glass windows, holds special symbolic importance.

Plate 26. El Escorial monastery
and palace (1563–84). El Escorial's
measurements, forms, and proportions
were intended to combine all the
millennia-old knowledge of Hermetic
architecture. The geometry of its lines
and spaces results from the use of
kabbalistic tools, alchemical principles,
Ramon Llull's mnemotechnics, and
Pythagorean numerology, among other
aspects of esotericism.

Plate 27. In order that there might be
no doubt as to the biblical inspiration of
El Escorial, Philip II had placed there
six great sculptures that represented the
Hebrew kings of the Hebrew scriptures:
Jehoshaphat, Manasseh, Josiah,
Hezekiah, David, and Solomon.

ate 28. In Gloria, *a fresco by Luca Cambiaso in the vault of El Escorial, we can*
the cube upon which are located, according to Hermetic tradition, the plans of the
mple of Solomon.

Plate 29. Villa Manin (late sixteenth century) in Passariano, Italy. Outside the city, Palladio built edifices that were not castles or fortresses but instead were spacious country residences of immortal beauty that existed in magical harmony with nature and with the universe itself.

Plate 30. Villa Barbaro (Maser, Italy). In 1551, Palladio built this villa that preserves the typical frontal design of Palladian villas: the central facade is a Greek temple with two stories and four columns, topped by an elegant triangular pediment.

Plate 31. In the eighteenth century, Villa Cornaro was the seat for the rituals of the first Italian Masonic lodge, whose members knew that this edifice was something more than just a pleasant country house.

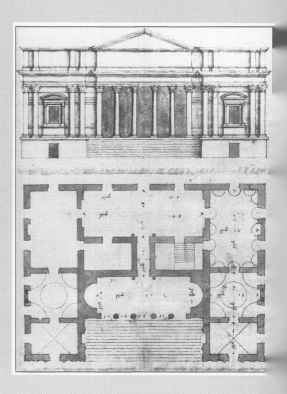

Plate 32. Original plans—the elevation and plan for the Villa Opere—by the architect Andrea Palladio.

*ate 33. Wolfgang Amadeus Mozart in 1784 (housed in Benevolencia, a Viennese
'asonic lodge). Even prior to this portrait, Mozart's flirtation with Masonry and
her Hermetic circles was reflected in various works, especially in* The Magic Flute
*791), which conceals beneath an innocent fable emblematic messages from Masonic
eology.*

Plate 34. Ludwig van Beethoven studied in Bonn under Christian Neefe, a confirmed Mason and probably a member of the secret sect known as the Illuminati. From 1781 to 1792, he was instilled with the Enlightenment's ideals of liberty and fraternity.

An Archaeological Enigma

Of course, the figure found at La Alcudia was not a Moorish queen from the African Maghreb, although it may show influences from the Punic and Carthaginian art brought to this region by Phoenician sailors. This possibility forms part of the bitter archaeological controversy surrounding the origin, antiquity, purpose, and even gender of the presumed lady. Its mystery has attained international dimensions because, shortly after its discovery, the proprietor of the estate, a physician named Campello, sold the statue to the French Hispanist Pierre Paris, who then gave it to the Louvre.

One of the first debates consisted of establishing the gender of this ambiguous face. The headdress and clothes appear feminine, but in ancient Mediterranean cultures men decorated themselves at least as much as women. In 1897, shortly after the statue's discovery, the municipal archivist Pedro Ibarra, a great enthusiast of archaeology, exhibited it at the Elche town hall as an image of the Apollonian god Mithras. The archaeologists did not accept this amateur opinion, but some admitted that the sculpture might be an androgynous figure. Later, the discovery of other similar pieces, especially the *Lady of Baza,*

The Lady of Baza *served as a reference for determining the gender of the* Lady of Elche.

confirmed that the Elche figure was truly a woman—but a woman of what class?

One version claimed that this was an Iberian representation of the goddess Tanit, a Punic version of the Phoenician Astarte, who in turn was the Ishtar of Sumer and Babylon. What is certain is that this deity, the protector of fertility and life, was worshipped by the Iberians and Turdetani of Phoenician origin who populated the southern portion of the peninsula. Other experts have observed that its features are similar to those of the feminine figures from the temple of Hera in Selinunte, Sicily, which represent the goddess herself and her Vestals. This would trace the statue's origins or influences to ancient Greek art and would explain the large coils on the head, which are common on other pieces from this culture.

In any case, there is considerable consensus that this is a statue of a goddess—probably a votive goddess. This opinion is supported by the hollow or hole in the back of the statue, which would have served for inserting votive objects. It was also the custom to offer the deity material gifts in the form of decorations or jewels for wearing. Wooden statues were often used for this purpose because they were easier to clothe and decorate than those made of stone. The explanation may be that the *Lady of Elche* was a copy of a wooden statue, commissioned as a grateful homage to a person or community and favored for its miraculous power.

Before concluding these considerations regarding the identity of the *Lady of Elche,* it is worth noting a recent and rather eccentric opinion: The American archaeologist John F. Moffit wrote an essay in 1995 entitled "Art Forgery: The Case of the Lady of Elche." This text, published by the University of Florida, claims to demonstrate that the piece and its discovery are fraudulent. Moffit was not alone in this denunciation; other authors have speculated the same—and the scientific community has not taken seriously these speculations.

The Lady's Movements

The *Lady of Elche* spent more than three decades in the Louvre until Franco negotiated with the Vichy government in 1941 to have the statue returned to Spain in exchange for some indeterminate favor. Exhibited in Madrid, the figure was one of the most admirable jewels in the Prado Museum until it was moved in 1971 to be exhibited in the National Archaeological Museum.

The leaders and citizens of Elche have always claimed that the *Lady* should return to its place of origin, where there is now an important deposit of archaeological pieces from the Iberian culture. But the authorities under both Franco and the democratic government have resisted these requests with a degree of centralism.

MICHELANGELO BUONARROTI
DAVID
(1501–4)

Celebrated as the most perfect work of art ever created, Michelangelo's *David* (now in the Accademia Gallery, Florence) may represent not only the biblical king of Israel but also the essential man aspired to by Renaissance philosophers. (See plate 20.)

The Mystery of the World's Most Beautiful Statue

The remarkable beauty and indefinable mystery of Michelangelo's *David* make it one of the most admirable masterpieces of all time. Any contemplation of it produces in the viewer a strange feeling of plenitude, as if its presence gives rise to a transcendental outburst that comes from another dimension. This aura of indefinable greatness has accompanied the statue since its creation, giving rise to praise from its devotees and furious attacks from its detractors. In neither case has anyone been able to judge it with indifference. Even in the sixteenth century the painter and critic Giorgio Vasari, in his famous biography of the great artists of the Renaissance, declared that *David* "took the voice away from all the statues ancient and modern, Greek or Roman, that have ever existed." Later experts and art historians have concurred in consecrating this work by Michelangelo as the most beautiful object that humanity has produced.

What inspired a young Florentine sculptor, twenty-six years old, to create this inimitable work? The answer may extend further than the technical skill, artistic talent, and creative imagination that characterized the great artists. Perhaps Michelangelo was predestined to create this perfect statue; one poet even said that perhaps it was David, that emblematic biblical king, who completed his own deeds by having Michelangelo sculpt him.

The Spirit of the Marble

On August 6, 1501, the chapter of the Florentine cathedral of Santa Maria del Fiore, known as Il Duomo, commissioned Michelangelo Buonarroti to make a statue of David to be placed in one of the alcoves formed by the buttresses of the cathedral's apse. The expenses were paid by the Arte della Lana, the woolen cloth guild that intended to offer this work as a homage to the Virgin Mary. Even from the beginning the wool guild did not seem very generous. They gave Michelangelo a piece of Carrara marble that had been rejected by two other sculptors because it was deemed too thin and fragile and had deep grooves that would have to be hidden with cement.

It is said that restrictions tend to stimulate artists' creativity—thus, Michelangelo was able to extract magnificent results from this imperfect, mistreated material. The block had a great hole at the bottom, which inspired the separation of the statue's legs: The weight is

View of the main facade of Santa Maria del Fiore, the original location of Michelangelo's David

placed on one of the legs and the other is flexed, in a new version of the *contrapposto* position of classical sculptures. The marble stopped at David's feet, however, with no room left for the head of the slaughtered Goliath. This problem determined the entire focus of the work: Because inclusion of Goliath's head was not an option, Michelangelo depicted the valiant shepherd at the moment of preparing to enter into combat with the giant. This decision went against every iconic tradition surrounding David, even that of Donatello, but it freed the work from an anecdotal detail that would have interfered with the appreciation of its grandeur.

Another inconvenience of the stone was the narrowing of the piece of marble near its top. The brilliant artist overcame this by carving David's head turned to one side, with his face engaged in a steady and direct stare, presumably fixed upon his opponent. This solution represented an innovation in the attitudes of individual sculptures, both classical and Renaissance.

It is certainly amazing that Michelangelo produced his marvelous work from such a defective piece of marble. Nevertheless, it was

The piece of marble was excessively narrow, but Michelangelo overcame this obstacle by sculpting David's head turned to one side.

his piece of marble—his and that of the form that struggled to manifest itself. The artists of the Renaissance, influenced by Erasmus of Rotterdam, believed that the marble contained the work of art just as the carnal body contained the spirit. The sculptor's mission was to extract the body and give it form.

Beyond King David

Described as the most beautiful and perfect expression of artistic creation, Michelangelo's *David* achieved this splendid description not through its anatomical perfection, which is incomplete, nor through its dimension as a work of art, which is indisputable. Critics have pointed out that the hands are excessively large in relation to the arms and the rest of the body; that the brow ridge, even though the subject is frowning, is too protuberant; and that there is a nonexistent muscle standing out from the left wrist. The disproportion of the hands may be due to the fact that the statue was originally intended to be placed high up, above the buttress of the apse. The artist may have opted to adapt its form for viewing from the ground, just as he did with the frescoes in the Sistine Chapel. Yet perhaps it must be accepted that these errors are simply due to the well-known axiom that nothing man-made is completely perfect.

The Florentine art of the Renaissance, inspired by Nicholas of Cusa and Marsilio Ficino, sought to find the *disegno,* the figure of the archetypal man, the Adamic model created by divine breath from the clay of Eden. Part of this search was the famous drawing by Leonardo da Vinci known as *Vitruvian Man:* a masculine nude inscribed simultaneously in a square and a circle. Several authors have suggested that Michelangelo's *David* represents not the Hebrew sovereign but this disegno, the essential and mysterious man of the Renaissance.

It is obvious that Michelangelo stripped his work of all the historical and legendary symbols attributed to its subject. Significant in itself is the absence of Goliath's head, an indispensable element for symbolizing this biblical story. Also absent, however, is any other accessory relating to this episode except for the slingshot David holds over his right shoulder. Even here, the artist did not chisel the object to look like a slingshot or like any other recognizable instrument. The weapon is simply a piece of material that cannot be defined, even though the sculpture was produced in highly skilled detail over a period of four years. The clerics and merchants who reviewed it saw it as David with his slingshot because this was what they had commissioned and what Michelangelo told them it represented.

A further question relates to the absolute nudity of the statue; the subject is devoid of even the most minimal garment or adornment. Although the Hebrew scriptures do suggest that the shepherd warrior was short on clothing—for before the fight he rids himself of the armor given him by Saul—the Book of Samuel also says that he took up his slingshot and shepherd's bag (I Samuel 17, 38–40), from which we may deduce that he was at least covered by a loincloth. Even though Michelangelo may have disdained the biblical source, representing the great king of Israel with his genitals in the open air was not necessarily irreverent. His patrons accepted it—albeit possibly with some embarrassment—with the Renaissance's professed immense respect for Greek art, whose masculine statues often showed their genitals. In any case, *David* was placed not in the cathedral but in the Piazza della Signoria, where it was later replaced with a copy while the original was moved to a room inside the Accademia Gallery to protect it from the weather.

During subsequent centuries this magnificent work continued to be known by the name of *David,* as did the numerous copies that exist throughout the world (some with the loins covered by a modest vine leaf)—but perhaps some initiated visitors contemplate the statue as the absolute man, created from Mother Earth with the image and seed of the gods.

BENVENUTO CELLINI
PERSEUS WITH THE HEAD OF MEDUSA
(1554)

The esoteric duke Cosimo de Medici commissioned this mythological work from Cellini. It conceals a Neoplatonic homage to Hermes Trismegistus and the female ancestral deities. (See color plate 21.)

The Primordial Hero and the Mother Goddess

More than ten feet tall, this striking bronze statue, now in the Loggia dei Lanzi, Florence, is among the few large pieces created by Cellini, who mainly worked as a goldsmith and medalist. Nonetheless, it is one of the most successful and striking monuments of the Italian Renaissance. The figure of Perseus, standing atop Medusa's slaughtered body and triumphantly holding up her bleeding head, presents an image of tremendous strength and terrible beauty.

The artist fell prey to great agitation and anxiety while he was executing Perseus with the Head of Medusa.

The subject of this sculpture was suggested to Cellini by Duke Cosimo I de Medici, the founder of the Florentine Academy and patron to Renaissance philosophers and intellectuals who promoted Platonic and Hermetic esotericism. These occultist currents had a great influence over the artists of the epoch, and many critics believe that in this sculpture, along with depicting a mythological scene, Cellini alluded to ancestral theogonies based on the primordial monster-slaying hero and the great goddess of the ancestral cults.

Some chroniclers from the time, and Cellini himself in his autobiography, have stated that during the execution of *Perseus with the Head of Medusa* the artist fell prey to great agitation and anxiety, as if the material he worked with resisted being forged in the way he wanted for this tremendous scene. The two mythical characters have an air of mystery and power that vies with those of their brilliant creator. Such was the anticipation created by this feverish anxiety that when the work was finally completed, there were celebrations and festivals all over Italy.

Perseus's Deed

In Greek mythology, Acrisius, king of Argos, was given a prophecy by the oracle foretelling that a future child of his daughter Danae would murder him. The king consequently locked the young woman in a bronze tower to prevent her from meeting men. Zeus, however, always ingenious, changed himself into a shower of gold that rained into the tower and impregnated Danae. The boy who was thus born was named Perseus—but his frightened grandfather shut the child and his mother in a wooden chest and cast them into the sea. Floating aimlessly, the chest reached the isle of Seriphos, ruled by the tyrant Polydectes.

Soon enough, Polydectes longed to marry the beautiful Danae and thought that Perseus might be an obstacle to this objective. The ruler therefore pretended that his betrothed was the princess Hippodamia and required Perseus to present a gift for the wedding. Because the youth had no possessions, he offered to bring the head of Medusa, one of the three Gorgon sisters and the only one of them who was mortal. This deadly trio had terrorized the people of all the islands in the Aegean Sea, for their gaze turned men into stone. No mortal had been able to defeat them, and Polydectes accepted Perseus's offer with satisfaction, certain that the youth would meet with the same stony fate as his predecessors. Little did the ruler know that the youth was a demigod and that Olympus had a surprise waiting for the tyrant.

According to the most popular description, the Gorgons had live, venomous snakes for hair; hands of metal; and sharp fangs—attributes that precluded their passing into the Hyperborean otherworld. Some sources present Medusa as a very beautiful, young, human female who had been violated by Poseidon in the temple of Athena. Enraged by this profanation, Athena turned her into the third Gorgon. Another version relates that Athena, envious of Medusa's splendid head of hair, changed it into a writhing mass of vipers.

When Perseus left in search of Medusa, his father Zeus decided to lend him a hand, ordering Athena and Hermes to help the youth in his enterprise. The god gave him a magic sword, and the goddess presented him with a mirrorlike shield and told him that the three Gray Sisters

Medusa and Perseus have been a recurring theme among great artists. The Gorgons changed men into stone with their stare. On the left is Caravaggio's Medusa; *on the right is a bust of Medusa by Lorenzo Bernini.*

knew the location of the Gorgons' lair. The hero sought out these three ancient witches and robbed them of the single eye that they took turns using. Terrified at being made blind, they confessed to him where the Gorgons were hiding in exchange for the return of their shared eye. Thus Perseus was able to take Medusa by surprise, and looking at her only in the mirror of his shield in order to avoid being petrified, he decapitated her with a single blow from the sword of Hermes. Cellini's sculpture shows him at this crucial moment, holding up the severed head as a triumphant trophy.

The Divided Goddess

The great statue of *Perseus with the Head of Medusa* may be, according to some critics, an homage to Duke Cosimo and his occultist protégés in the world of magic and Hermeticism. Cellini's choice to sculpt this scene was due not only to his great artistic gifts but also to his contact with the Platonic Academy and esoteric ideas. The occult significance of the monument leads back to the primordial chaos from which emerged the creator gods and their prototypes. The primary deity was an androgynous and omniscient being who separated into the two genders as Creation stagnated. The female part was the goddess of the serpents, a phallic symbol representing not the penis but fertilizing power. In primitive cultures this goddess was worshipped as Mother Earth (and the mother of all goddesses), in ancient Egypt she took the form of Isis, and in Mesopotamia she was Ishtar and Astarte.

Little by little, the supremacy of men in vital activities such as hunting and war produced an advance on the part of the male god, which grew with Akhenaten and Moses as monotheism emerged. The worship of the mother goddess was reduced and the feminine deities retained only secondary roles as wives, mothers, and daughters of the great, virile gods. For the Greeks, the great goddess was divided into two figures of differing origin: Athena Parthenos, a Cretan and Etruscan goddess, and the Serpent Goddess of the Amazon nomads of Anatolia whom the Achaeans called Medusa. In Attic mythology, the two are sisters, both enemies and accomplices: the martial Athena, goddess of wisdom, strategist and warrior, and the terrible Medusa, who is her shadow because she is dark and ethereal. Athena, however, carries a shield, and on her belt buckle is the image of Medusa's head with its serpents, a talisman to protect against the demons of the otherworld (an amulet also worn by Alexander the Great).

A Secret Homage

Medusa and her Gorgon sisters were three of the Hyperborean monsters that lived in caves and subterranean galleries beyond the northern limit of the world. They were malignant creatures that threatened humans with their horrible weapons (claws, fiery tongues, venomous fangs, devastating eyes, etc.). From the mists of antiquity there sprang forth epic characters who were capable of fighting and killing these monsters and liberating from them all terrified people. Perseus was the Greek version of this revered leader, and he was transformed by medieval Christianity into the dragon-slaying St. George—who has nothing to do with Don Quixote, who tilted at the windmills of La Mancha, mistaking them for terrible giants.

Perseus, however, was only an adolescent demigod who needed the help of Athena; she gave him her protecting shield to assist him in conquering Medusa. The god who gave him the magic sword, though, was none other than the thrice-great Hermes, alleged author of the *Corpus Hermeticum* and inspirer of all the occult sciences studied by the Florentine Neoplatonists. Erecting a monument to Perseus may have been, in the eyes of Cosimo and the members of his Academy, a secret homage to Hermes Trismegistus for having armed the warrior who destroyed the monster of shadows and her venomous serpents.

ARCHITECTURE

rchitecture is the only art form that emerged as the result of a concrete necessity for survival—from the construction of habitable shelters to protect humans from inclement weather and the threat of wild beasts. Gradually, in Egyptian and Mediterranean cultures the shacks and hovels of prehistoric times were replaced with artistic buildings in the first Neolithic cities. Houses, squares, temples, ziggurats, pyramids, mausoleums, and other buildings acquired increasingly complex and elaborate structure and production. Architects and master builders attained a superior status, which was at times comparable to that of mages and priests, for they were creators and thaumaturges in the most visible sense of these terms.

In the societies of antiquity, the gods needed "houses" just as people did—residences where they could be invoked and worshipped. Further, the worship of ancestors required monumental sepulchres and pantheons built according to strict rules. In some ways, these edifices were impregnated with the superhuman powers of their intangible residents, and as a result architecture became a kind of sacred art that assumed the command of Hermetic knowledge.

Almost all the religions that emerged throughout history maintained these dwellings of the gods as well as the sacredness of tombs and cemeteries. The same phenomenon occurred in monotheistic religions in the form of synagogues, mosques, and Christian churches.

Their builders made an effort to give them solemnity and beauty but also to preserve certain rules and secret symbols that would instill the faithful who frequented them with a magical feeling of elevation and mysticism.

The mysterious character of architecture was not limited to its religious component. Secret orders constructed cathedrals into which were built Hermetic symbols and secrets, kings constructed palaces with esoteric references, and architects designed residences specifically according to the Hermetic norms of Pythagorean mathematicians. Here we can see a few examples of the occult side of certain works of architecture.

HEMON (EGYPTIAN ARCHITECT)
GREAT PYRAMID OF CHEOPS
(ca. 2570 BCE)

This pyramid, the only remaining wonder of the Seven Wonders of the Ancient World and located in the Valley of Giza, conceals within its enigmatic perfection all the esoteric knowledge of the Egyptian priests and mages and its intent of ruling heaven and earth. (See color plate 22.)

The Magical Axis of the World

Buildings in pyramidal form descend from an extremely ancient tradition of transcendence and mystery. Their construction and veneration took place in a wide range of cultures: from the terraced ziggurats dedicated to the Sumerian and Babylonian gods and the Egyptian pyramids to those of pre-Columbian Mexico, Southeast Asia, and Oceania. All shared similar proportions and were consecrated as sacred temples or tombs for revered rulers. Priests and astrologers of pagan cults believed that this polyhedral shape possessed mysterious powers. Inside a pyramid it was easier to communicate with the gods, enter into mystical ecstasies, and invoke mysterious forces in initiatory rituals, divinatory trances, and funereal ceremonies.

This magical prestige was maintained over time by Pythagorean geometricians, mages, and medieval alchemists and by various healers and diviners who used smaller pyramids to heal the sick and predict the future. The largest such structure recently built is the great crystal pyramid at the entrance to the Louvre. Placed in an inverted position, it perhaps indicates the subterranean path that leads to the Hermetic symbols in the great works of art housed there—the kind of symbols that are the subject of this book.

The Pharaoh's Pyramid

Among the pyramids that have survived to our times, the most imposing, mysterious, and perfect is indisputably that of Cheops, standing in the Valley of Giza. This pharaoh of the autocratic Fourth Dynasty initiated by his father, Snefru, ruled from 2604 to 2581 BCE. Not much is known about him except that he brought an era of great power and splendor to Egypt—and, of course, that he had the famous pyramid built. According to legend, he enslaved the entire population to work on its immense construction and even prostituted his own daughter to gain the copious funds necessary.

The work of construction took about twenty years, during which time, depending on the source consulted, between 100,000 and 350,000 men were employed. The planning and direction of the construction were in the hands of the architect Hemon, a relative of the pharaoh.

The pyramid's colossal dimensions put the peak at about 480 feet, making it taller than any monument ever built previously. Each of the four sides of the base measures exactly 755.84 feet, making for a total surface area of more than 571,000 square feet. It has been calculated that to build the pyramid roughly 2.5 million square stone blocks were required, each weighing approximately 2.2 tons, although some of the blocks weighed as much as 66 tons. These cubic stones are joined so perfectly that tourists cannot even fit their credit cards into the cracks between them. Originally, the triangular walls were covered with 25,000 white stone plaques, now lost, which must have been blinding in the light of the sun.

The colossal structure is located exactly on the 30th parallel of north latitude, at its intersection with the meridian of 31 degrees east, which divides the earth's landmasses into two equal parts. The pyramid's shape preserves the 3-4-5 proportions attributed to the magic triangle of alleged antediluvian origin and later applied by Pythagoras to his esoteric geometry.

Another version of the story claims that the Great Pyramid had already been built before Cheops's accession to the throne, and that he only had himself buried in it. If this was so, he must at least have added the mortuary chamber and several other rooms, for every self-respecting pharaoh had to build his own monumental sepulchre or else be doomed to wander endlessly through the world of the dead. Placing the sepulchre of the pharaoh deep within the pyramid was a tradition connected to the necrophilia practiced in Egyptian cults. The transition from life to death required a series of rituals, including mummification and the placement in the sarcophagus of a number of provisions for the voyage. Kings were provided with objects to help lift the spirit through the apex of the pyramid, where they would meet with the sun god, Amon-Ra, the greatest deity of Egyptian theogony who guided souls to eternal repose.

The pyramid of Cheops in itself expresses all the mysterious secrets of ancient Egypt and is amazingly finely preserved, having deteriorated very little over the millennia—for, as Egyptian guides often repeat to tourists, time conquers all things, but the Great Pyramid of Cheops conquers time.

Various authors have questioned how, in less than a century, the Egyptians made the leap from elementary mastabas and pyramids made of sticks, straw, and mortar to such a solid and sophisticated structure. It is not understood how, without having wheels, they managed to transport the stone from more than six hundred miles away; nor is it known how they cut the stone into blocks, raised each more than three hundred feet, and placed each in precise position without the use of cranes or pulleys. Above all, many have asked why the Egyptians situated the Great Pyramid and the other two pyramids in the Valley of Giza at precisely the same proportional distances and angles found among the three main stars in the constellation Orion.

The Soul of the World

The pyramid of Cheops has drawn the attention of numerous astronomers, geometricians, parapsychologists, astrologers, and, of course, occultists of various leanings who have studied its proportions, enclosures, and curious relationship to terrestrial measurements and celestial movements. According to them, this is not merely a material monument but also a kind of immobile organism that emits enigmatic vibrations and produces strange psychic and physical reactions in visitors. They claim that these phenomena have been proved with scientific measuring instruments and corroborated by those who have no connection to esotericism. Upon entering the interior space of the pyramid, some people have claimed to suffer from breathlessness, dizziness, and even fainting. Scientists attribute these reactions to the sensation of being closed in and to the rarefaction of the air in the structure, although their opponents argue that these effects are not nearly so obvious in any other similar environment, nor do other similar spaces cause the same auditory hallucinations. According to some testimonies, in the galleries of the pyramid there can be heard voices and strange sounds that do not have any human or material cause.

The first scientist to announce another extraordinary power of the Great Pyramid was the French archaeologist André de Bovis, who found in the mortuary chamber an entirely mummified cat that looked just like a living animal. De Bovis stated that he had brought another cat that had just died into the same chamber, and after a few weeks it was in the same mummified state as the original cat found there. He tried this with other animals—vertebrates and fish—and became persuaded that despite the high humidity in the interior, the pyramid emanated something unknown that prevented putrefaction and quickly

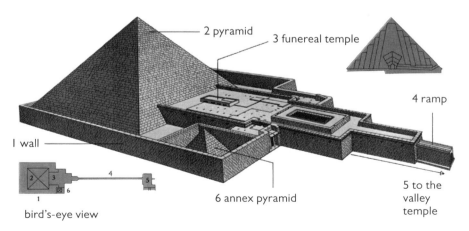

1 wall
2 pyramid
3 funereal temple
4 ramp
5 to the valley temple
6 annex pyramid
bird's-eye view

Plan of a classic pyramid like the Great Pyramid

dessicated organic tissues, producing results much like those seen in the millennia-old cadavers found in glaciers or at the tops of high mountains. This macabre force has also been attributed to the Mexican pyramid of Teotihuacan and may result from an electromagnetic effect produced by certain pyramidal forms. According to this theory, electromagnetism reacts with the telluric vibrations of the subsoil, thus giving rise to an intense wave that has the ability to slowly mummify dead bodies.

Because this magnetism corresponds to the color of negative green in the spectrum, its discoverers have called it the green ray. Decipherers of hieroglyphs have found symbols that may mean something like "green power," which suggests that the demiurgic Egyptian priests knew the effects of electromagnetism, and perhaps also electricity, which would have had an exclusively magical function for them. This idea has been confirmed by objects that are often found placed on top of empty sarcophagi in the kings' chambers. These objects have a structure similar to a beehive, built with four overlapping sections. Some authorities suggest that this was a battery that emitted strong invisible waves corresponding to negative green.

Recognition of these facts swings between the reticence of scientists and the imagination of esoteric investigators. If we remain true to the significance of the Great Pyramid in terms of the beliefs of its time of construction, then we can conclude that it was at once a temple, a pantheon, a mummification studio, and an astral laboratory. Through it the terrestrial was linked to the cosmic, and its forms gave rise to a mystical rebirth. The priests and astrologers knew it as the soul of the world.

ANONYMOUS GOTHIC ART
CHARTRES CATHEDRAL
(TWELFTH–THIRTEENTH CENTURIES)

This Gothic cathedral in Chartres, France, built on the site of a magical Druid sanctuary, represents an inexplicable advancement in construction techniques and has an enigmatic Templar connection, which together form a great deal of Hermetic knowledge. (See color plate 23.)

The Great Temple of the Templars

The ancient Celts, who knew and worshipped the powers of nature, set up their mystical centers at sites favorable to telluric magnetism. One of the most important of these was on the plain of Beauce, in the northeast of present-day France, some fifty miles from Lutetia (Paris), where a prehistoric dolmen was discovered. This primitive structure, built on a rise in the land, was formed by three vertical monoliths covered by a flat, horizontal stone. In ancient times, the Druids had dug a well down to where they found a subterranean current that produced strong telluric vibrations. Convinced that it was an especially propitious site for mystic meditation and spiritual elevation, they dedicated the place to the magic rituals and ceremonies of their religious cults. Later, near this sanctuary they also built a study center for the initiation of priests and demiurges.

Today, rising in this spot is the magnificent cathedral of Our Lady of Chartres, a masterpiece of Gothic architecture and the first European cathedral to be dedicated to the adoration of the Virgin Mary. These qualities alone have made it an emblem of Christianity for centuries, as well as a center for artistic interest and religious pilgrimages. Chartres, however, has other, less obvious attractions connected to the Hermetic tradition, esoteric Christianity, and the ancient secrets possessed by the Templars.

Secret Architecture

The Order of the Temple was inspired by Bernard of Clairvaux, one of the most enigmatic saints in Christian hagiography. He was a monk who left the Order of Cluny to join in the founding of the Cistercian Order, which made him abbot of the Clairvaux abbey. This new order believed in austerity, the original doctrines of early Christianity as applied through the severe Rule of St. Benedict, and the preservation of Hermetic knowledge. In 1118, Bernard gathered some French knights to form the Order of the Temple in Jerusalem, which was ruled at the time by Crusaders.

Perhaps it was no coincidence that the Templars' first seat was next to the ruins of the Temple of Solomon. It is said that they found underground cellars and passages and, within them, invaluable ancient Hebrew treasures such as the Ark of the Covenant, documents recording esoteric knowledge from the great biblical king Solomon, and secret architectural plans and standards used in the construction of his Temple. It is possible that Bernard knew this from his mysterious erudition and that his intent was to recover these items and knowledge and bring them to Europe to unite them with the traditions of Celtic magic and the Arthurian legend of the Holy Grail, thereby forming a Hermetic ensemble known as the Great Secret.

What is certain is that shortly after the founding of the Order of the Temple, the first Gothic cathedrals appeared in France, representing a leap in architecture so great that it cannot be explained solely by the technical and structural advances of the so-called twelfth-century Renaissance. Various authors, including the recognized expert Louis Charpentier, state that during this time the Templars and the Cistercians must have formed an alliance that launched a program for the building of enormous cathedrals with vertically rising facades and much more complex structures and decorations than were found in the austere Roman churches and cathedrals.

The Templars reached their high point simultaneously with the rise of the Gothic cathedrals. Not counting the great Cistercian abbeys that

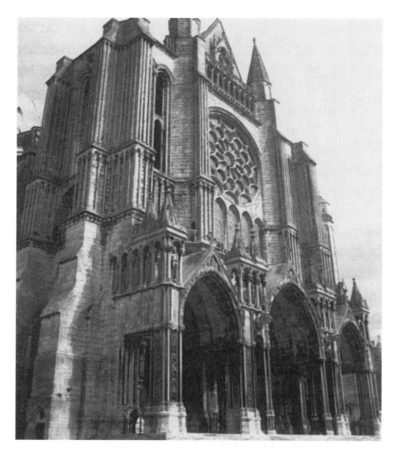

The main facade of Chartres Cathedral: All the spaces and surfaces of the edifice, as well as the proportions and distances between them, obey the rule of the golden section, or golden ratio (1.61803), which was considered magical by the Pythagoreans and the Hermetic sciences.

were built in the same style, only in France were more than eight of these structures built in a century. Chartres Cathedral was erected precisely on the energetic point of the previous Celtic sanctuaries. At the time, Chartres was a town with only five thousand inhabitants, and the choice of this location for building the cathedral was explained by presenting as necessary the rebuilding of the Roman cathedral that had stood there before and had been accidentally destroyed by a mysterious fire in 1193. The new cathedral was begun in the following year. In a few months, the necessary materials were carried to Chartres, and dozens of specialized workers came to the town, perhaps thanks to the Templars' strong connections to the lodges of the stone workers. The work was finished in only thirty years—record time for this era—with later additions and alterations leading to its definitive completion in 1290.

Chartres was the first edifice supported by a system of flying buttresses: external pillars that relieve the walls from having to support the entire weight of the structure. This technique allowed for slender, ogival windows in the facade (another novelty) and allowed the naves of the church to be inundated with colored light that shone through the immense stained-glass rose and triforium windows. The other great innovation of Chartres was the peaked vault, supported by visible ribs intersecting with each other to distribute the weight. The Templars, who directed and financed the work, may have gained this remarkable knowledge from the *Golden Book of Wisdom,* a mysterious esoteric volume containing Hermetic secrets having to do with kabbalistic numerology and its application to a system of weights and measures. All the spaces and surfaces of the cathedral, as well as the proportions and distances between them, obey the rule of the so-called golden ratio, or golden section (1.61803), which is considered magical by both Pythagoreans and Hermetic scientists. For example, all the distances between the pillars are multiples of this number, as are the lengths of the central nave, transepts, and choir and the proportions of the spaces and surfaces of the entire structure.

The Esoteric Symbols

Within the structure of the cathedral the Templars and Cistercians planted an entire program of esoteric symbols for the initiated that were designed to be as eternal as the church's stones cut by the masons. This system comprised distances, the handling of light, the position of the vault, the relief carvings, the stained-glass of the windows, and the layout of the flagstones on the floor. Many of these elements were lost in later renovations and additions and even through the actions of vandals, but there are still enough of them left—as can be seen from a simple visit to the cathedral—to confirm the presence of this Hermetic legacy.

The mystical and transcendent center of Chartres is located between the second and third rows of the choir, where the original altar stands. This point is directly above the Druids' subterranean well, which is 120 feet deep—exactly the same as the distance from the floor to the pinnacle of the vault. This significant distance also corresponds to the width of the central nave. It is believed that the interaction between the telluric forces of the well and the cosmic vibrations attracted by the spire creates a special magnetic field that spreads throughout the interior of the nave. According to numerous testimonies, those who enter the cathedral can sense the effects of this interaction in the form of an intense sensation of peace and spiritual elevation.

On June 21 of each year, a ray of sun shines through a small piece of transparent crystal in the window of St. Apollinare and directly lights a flagstone in the west wing of the south transept. Strangely, this flagstone is the only one placed obliquely to all the others. June 21 is the date of the summer solstice, a symbol of the rebirth of life in almost all the pagan cults. It is a date that was celebrated by the Celts and coincides with what Catholics observe as the feast of St. John. This slanting flagstone undoubtedly once concealed something—a relic, a document, or a magical talisman that was removed or destroyed at some point in its long history.

The Circular Labyrinth

In the middle of the great central corridor leading to the transept, the flagstones on the floor form a circular labyrinth that is almost 40 feet in diameter and dates to the original thirteenth-century construction. Such labyrinths, typical sources of vibrations in the Hermetic symbology used by the Templars, can be seen in other Gothic cathedrals, although Chartres's labyrinth is the only one that is well preserved today. It is made up of eleven concentric circular rings that are connected to each other in such a way that those walking the labyrinth can traverse

The mysterious circular labyrinth of Chartres Cathedral

a complete distance of almost 860 feet. It has been documented that in the Middle Ages the villagers of Chartres shuffled along the paths of the labyrinth on their knees when cold or snow prevented them from completing their penances outside. It is also said that Templar knights and initiated monks came to the cathedral to perform certain secret ceremonies in the energetic field of the labyrinth.

The Ark of the Covenant
Other indubitably Templar symbols can be found in two small pillars near the statue of the Queen of Sheba by the north gate, also known

as the Gate of the Initiated. One of the pillars bears a relief showing the Ark of the Covenant being transported on a cart; the other shows a man covering the Ark and a pile of dead bodies with a veil. Among these is a Templar knight with his chain-mail coat. On the bases of the two pillars, an inscription in the stone reads *Hic amititur Arca cederis,* which means nothing in Latin. Some scholars claim this reading of the inscription is incorrect; either the engraver made an error or centuries of erosion have made it impossible to read correctly. They suggest that the original was meant to be *Hic amicitur Arca foederis,* which means "Here the Ark of the Covenant is hidden."

We must remember that the Templars are credited with finding the Ark in Jerusalem. According to tradition, it was discovered buried beneath the stables of the Temple of Solomon, and the order's most important mission was to protect it and prevent it from falling into profane hands. The Templars, the secret builders of Chartres Cathedral, may have hidden the Ark between the walls of the edifice in a place where only they could access it via an initiatory portal. The reliefs showing the Ark being transported on a cart and a knight covering the bodies of the men who died in the enterprise agree with the reading of the inscription proposed by scholars. Further confirmation of this is the proximity to the pillars of the statue of the Queen of Sheba, the African priestess who was an ally and lover of King Solomon.

A secret message, undoubtedly from the Templars, can be seen in these two small columns.

The Cult of the Black Virgin

When the Romans discovered the Druidic sanctuary at Chartres in the third century, they found there a wood carving of a woman with a child in her arms. The statue was made of pear-tree wood that had been blackened by the passage of time and by smoke from rituals, or perhaps by fire. Later, the Christians assumed that this was a carving of the Virgin Mary, who was said to have revealed herself to the French in a series of frequent miraculous apparitions. Thus began the cult of the Black Virgin, also known as the Subterranean Virgin or Virgo Partitura because of the newborn child she held in her arms. In their syncretism with Christianity, pagans adopted her as a new version of the ancestral mother goddess or Mother Earth, who played a role in almost all known theogonies.

Within the Catholic Church, the Black Virgin received a veneration that was suspected of heterodoxy due to the actions and characteristics attributed to her. Yet her worship has extended to churches and congregations all over the world and numerous images exist of the Virgo Partitura with her dark skin. She is generally sheltered in sanctuaries located in grottoes or hidden places, such as the underground crypt above the Druids' Well upon which Chartres Cathedral was built.

In Spain, there is a Black Virgin in Catalonia, at the top of the strange, steep rock formation of Montserrat, where there stands an eleventh-century Benedictine monastery. Here, people come to venerate the miraculous Moreneta, the popular name for Our Lady of Montserrat, whose image has been present in a grotto on the mountain since the year 880.

MAURICE DE SULLY (SPONSOR)
NOTRE DAME DE PARIS
(TWELFTH–THIRTEENTH CENTURIES)

Throughout history, the greatest master alchemists viewed this Parisian cathedral on the Place du Parvis, Île de la Cité, Paris, as a stone encyclopedia of this occult science. The writer Victor Hugo attempted to translate it through the gargoyle eyes of his famous hunchback. (See color plate 24.)

Our Lady of Alchemy

The famous and beautiful Notre Dame de Paris is an early Gothic edifice that presents all the perfect equilibrium of structure and the complex external and internal decoration that characterized this style. Its facade, flanked by two gates, with three porticoes and a great rose window at its center, formed the model for later churches and served as the archetype of the Gothic cathedral. Like other ecclesiastical works from this period, it was built over the ruins of a Roman sanctuary, which was established on one of the ritual sites of the Gaulish Druids. Work on the cathedral, sponsored by Maurice de Sully, bishop of Paris, was begun in 1163. The name of the architect is no longer known, but it is believed that the prelate himself supervised the design and construction. The building was completed in just over eighty years—a relatively short amount of time for this kind of undertaking—and was concluded in 1245 with the completion of the west facade. Shortly afterward, during the reign of Louis IX, the architects Jean Chelles and Pierre de Montreuil extended the two arms of the transept, augmenting both of them with new porticoes and splendid rose windows and also adding a new series of chapels on the north side. Thus the cathedral acquired its full splendor and the mystical aura that gives its form such magnificence.

Besides being important as a Christian cathedral, Notre Dame has always fascinated the devotees of esotericism, especially those adept in alchemy. From the point of view of this esoteric science, the cathedral is a veritable stone encyclopedia whose secret pages can be read only by the initiated. A mysterious tradition relates that medieval alchemists used to meet in the right-hand portico, where, aided by the energy of this magical and sacred edifice, they exchanged recipes and devised techniques.

The Petrified Alchemist

The idea that Notre Dame is a temple dedicated to alchemy has had various followers throughout history. Guillaume de Paris in the thirteenth century, Nicholas Flamel in the fifteenth century, Gobineau de Montluisant in the seventeenth century, and Victor Hugo in the nineteenth century all paved the way for the emergence of the mysterious twentieth-century initiate Fulcanelli. Possessing great erudition and exceptional intelligence, Fulcanelli was admired by the initiated and the profane alike for his famous book, *Le mystère des cathédrales,* published in 1929. In this book, Fulcanelli supports his theories with a detailed and clever study of the alchemical symbols and codes that can be clearly observed at Notre Dame de Paris—and he does so with such brilliance that even positivist academics and many ecclesiastical authorities have been forced to recognize his talent.

One of the most remarkable things about Fulcanelli was that he carried out his rigorous investigations without renouncing esotericism. Another was his analysis of a carving found in the second gallery of the great cathedral and known as The Old Man of Stone. According to Fulcanelli, this was a great medieval master alchemist who had obtained the formula for petrifying himself while he was alive. This alchemist's intent—according to Fulcanelli—was to remain there for eternity, awaiting the initiates who would, as time passed, understand his Hermetic message.

Among other reliefs and carvings to which Fulcanelli attributes alchemical significance, he singles out the medallion in the atrium of the center portico (the portal of the Last Judgment), above a column

The Old Man of Stone, according to the learned Fulcanelli, was a great alchemist who petrified himself while he was alive in order to remain in the cathedral for eternity, awaiting the initiates who would be able to understand his Hermetic message.

on the left side. This carving shows a woman seated in an ornate arm-chair, holding in her right hand an open book and a closed book and in her left a scepter. Above her is a vertical brick staircase and behind her head flows a current of water. The allusions to alchemy are obvious, even to the greatest skeptic: The closed book represents esoteric knowledge and the open book represents exoteric knowledge; the staircase, with nine steps, represents the path that must be followed upward in order to achieve the Great Work; the waters represent the Hermetic formula for mercury; and the scepter depicts the alchemical dominion over life and the universe.

Victor Hugo's Hunchback

The most famous work of fiction related to Notre Dame de Paris is the novel published under the title *Notre Dame de Paris* in 1831 and better known as *The Hunchback of Notre Dame*. The spirit of Romanticism had gathered medieval legends and mysteries, and Hugo masterfully combined the enigma of the Gothic cathedral and the occultism of alchemy.

The protagonist is Quasimodo, a hunchbacked peasant who lives hidden in the nooks and crannies of the cathedral, suffering from his unrequited love for a beautiful Gypsy girl. The author dedicated an entire chapter (book 5, chapter 2) to presenting his idea that architecture is a sacred art in which can be read the occult history of humanity. According to him, this great stone narrative was cut short by the invention of the printing press and the widespread distribution of profane books.

Victor Hugo's central idea was that the Gothic cathedrals represented the culmination of this mysterious architecture whose message contained a significant degree of liberty: "This liberty goes very far. Sometimes a portal, a facade, an entire church presents a symbolical sense absolutely foreign to worship or even hostile to the Church." His romantic narrative proceeded with many ups and downs. One critic went so far as to suggest that Quasimodo represented the stone alchemist or a hideous gargoyle that was incarnated within him.

Monsters Lying in Wait

A visitor to Notre Dame who looks skyward will discover that all the way up to the tops of the towers and the edges of the roof tops are perched countless ghastly, demonic monsters. These are examples of the famous Gothic gargoyles, nightmarish creatures seated on the drainpipes of cathedrals and other buildings from this era. The idea of extending the mouths of drainpipes and rain gutters was used in Egyptian, Greek, Etruscan, and Roman architecture. The gutters that caught the rain that ran over the roof tiles were extended with pipes

The gargoyles of Notre Dame are enigmatic and grim sculptures. According to some, their function is merely decorative; others claim they can be interpreted as demonic symbols.

made of stone or mortar in order to stop the water from trickling down the walls of a structure. In the twelfth century, stone workers began carving figures in the blocks intended for this purpose, freely using their imaginations.

The first gargoyles, in the form of fantastical and infernal animals, appeared on the upper reaches of Notre Dame and lent a grim air to this part of the cathedral. Although other cathedrals and significant buildings in the High Middle Ages followed this example, the series at Notre Dame is considered the most varied and artistic in the genre because no two gargoyles are alike and because their originality and expressiveness make them true works of art. Experts have not been able to agree on the reason or meaning behind these stone monsters: Some insist that they are merely eccentric roof decorations, while others see them as a blatant expression of demonic messages in Gothic artwork.

In the major renovation carried out by the architect Viollet-le-Duc in the fourteenth century, many false gargoyles, known as *chimeras,* were added. These carvings were placed in the same areas as the original gargoyles, but none of their mouths were connected to drainpipes. The chimeras, therefore, have no functional reason for being where they are and are purely artistic decorations. Most of them are anthropomorphic animals with human heads, or vice versa, adding to the cathedral's repertoire of stony monstrosities. Their mute and elevated presence forms a sort of diabolical guard that watches over one of Christianity's greatest temples.

More Esotericism

Alchemy is not the only type of Hermetic knowledge concealed beneath the face of Notre Dame. Seventeenth-century astrologers established that if we draw imaginary lines joining France's seven principal Gothic cathedrals, the resulting illustration outlines the constellation of Orion, with each cathedral representing one of its stars. The one exception to this is the cathedral in Paris, which is located at the exact center of this astral design.

There is more: The great rose window on the west side (see color plate 25) has at its center an image of the Virgin Mary dressed in a green tunic covered with a red cloak. These colors go against all iconographic tradition; Mary, the mother of Jesus, has always been depicted with a blue cloak over a white or light-colored tunic. As it happens, however, red is a highly significant color in occultism: It is the most powerful of the three alchemical colors (the other two being white and black), and with the green of the tunic, it forms a pair of colors that was highly symbolic for the Masons. In Ancient Scottish and Accepted Freemasonry, the sanctuary where the degree of the Knight of the Grand Orient and the Sword is confirmed contains two ritual areas: one of red and one of green.

Nor is paganism absent from the mysteries of this imposing Gothic monument. During the renovations of 1711, two thick walls were partially demolished, and behind these were found a number of statues that bore no resemblance to medieval religious sculpture. Arranged in a line, they depicted half-naked women and men with a strange appearance. They represented pagan deities such as Minerva, Mars, Apollo, Diana, Mercury, and Venus, and, according to archaeologists, they came from an ancient Roman temple dedicated to Jupiter and dating from the first century CE.

Notre Dame de Paris stands on an island in the midst of the city and is flanked by two channels of the Seine. To get there, a visitor must cross the waters, an essential initiatory act in many ancient cults and old religions, from the biblical crossing of the Red Sea and the Hindu sacred bathing in the Ganges to the Essene baptism in the Jordan and, symbolically, the Christian sacrament of baptism. Rivers and water also have metaphorical significance in the kabbalah and in other currents of esoteric knowledge. In alchemy, water represents the liquefaction of mercury, the first step along the path of the Great Work. In mainland cultures, islands have always maintained a certain degree of mystery and occult power; they have been both feared and venerated at the same time. Perhaps for this reason the Place du Parvis in front of Notre Dame was marked as Kilometer 0, the beginning spot for all roads leaving Paris.

JUAN BAUTISTA DE TOLEDO AND JUAN DE HERRERA (ARCHITECTS) EL ESCORIAL MONASTERY AND PALACE (1563–84)

In El Escorial, in San Lorenzo de El Escorial, Madrid, the intent of Philip II was to rebuild the legendary Temple of Solomon using Hermetic knowledge and secret techniques of construction based on ancient architecture with a divine origin. (See color plate 26.)

A Mystic and Esoteric Monument

From the mystical and esoteric point of view, the monastery of El Escorial is one of the most remarkable existing works of ecclesiastic architecture. It was built by order of Philip II in celebration of the 1557 victory of San Quintín, at which Spanish troops defeated Admiral Gaspard de Coligny, the leader of the French Huguenots. The Spanish king was a fervent Catholic and thus perhaps it was no coincidence that he built an elaborate ecclesiastical monument to celebrate his victory over an army that fought on the side of the Reformation. His essential intent, however, was to erect a symbolic reproduction of the destroyed Temple of Solomon (a monarch with whom he liked to compare himself), a sort of Civitate Dei, a mystical center of the world and an emblem of the reunification of Christianity over which he hoped to preside.

A Mystical Work in a Magical Place

The obsessive mysticism of Philip II manifested itself in a kind of double life. In public, he appeared as an austere and severe Catholic monarch who presided over the judgments and executions of the Inquisition, but in private, he surrounded himself with astrologers, gnostics, and kabbalists. The most influential among these was Benito Arias Montano, an intellectual, translator, polyglot, erudite, and member of the secret society known as the Sons of God. This group of scholars practiced a sort of Christian kabbalism that was dedicated to a certain interpretation of the Bible and was connected to King Solomon, an interest that led them to mingle with the Jewish Tadea Tecta (covered lamp) sect and perhaps with the Order of the Temple, which lived on within the Order of St. James.

It was possibly Montano who, even before the battle of San Quintín, suggested to Philip II the place where the king should build his monastic monument. El Escorial (The Slag Heap), as its name indicates, was raised on a bed of slag deposits that the locals called "the gate of hell," located at the foot of Mount Abanto on the Guadarrama Sierra, at an elevation of about 3,200 feet some thirty miles from Madrid. At the time, nothing was located there but a modest country house, found at the exact geographical center of the Iberian Peninsula and on the same parallel that passes through Rome.

Despite its function as a garbage dump, the place had held a certain mysterious fame since ancient times, for currents of water ran beneath the ground there and formed an extensive subterranean aquifer. The Celtic Druids, medieval alchemists, and Arab mages all considered these currents to have special vibrations, and the Moors called this region Mah'rit, "place of hidden waters," which later became the name Madrid.

Once the site had been chosen for the monastery, the planning was assigned to the architect Juan Bautista de Toledo, who also had esoteric inclinations. Both he and his fame had reached as far as Rome, where he had been a disciple of Michelangelo. Advised by Montano, he drew the square ground plan, which included the monastery and the church. In 1563 the plans were approved and the preparation of the site and transportation of materials began, but Toledo died four years later without having begun the building.

The construction fell to the hands of the secondary architect, Juan de Herrera, who, like his predecessor, was no stranger to the Hermetic arts. An expert in mystical architecture and a scholar of necromancy—divination performed by consulting the dead—he possessed a collection of talismanic stones and metals, conducted spells, and was probably a

Mason. More than two centuries later, the famous architect Ventura Rodriguez wrote in a letter to Francisco de Goya: "When the great architect Herrera was studying in the lodge of Trasmiera, whose meetings took place in Santa Maria de Bareyo, this was not the only Masonic work occupying his efforts. He also practiced the Royal Art, leading King Philip through the ways of the Majorcan [Ramon Llull] in search of the Great Work." Even if we ignore the temptation to consider all architects as probable Masons, Rodriguez certainly provided very precise information, such as the name of Herrera's lodge and the location of its meetings. The astrologer and palmist Matías Haco Sumbergense was also a member of this courtly circle; he was the author of the horoscope of Philip II known as El Prognosticón, and he calculated the orientation of El Escorial in relation to the celestial spheres.

And so here we have a king inclined toward esotericism, an intellectual inclined toward the occult sciences, an architect and Mason following Ramon Llull's Neoplatonic Hermeticism, and an astrologer with gifts of divination getting ready to raise nothing less than the new Temple of Solomon in the sierra outside Madrid.

A Monastery for the Holy Grail

The building's inauguration ceremony, during which the king symbolically laid the first stone, took place on June 23. This date was not random, but instead was chosen ahead of time as the day of St. Lawrence, to whom the monastery was dedicated. Nor was the choice of this patron saint arbitrary, considering that in Christian hagiography Lawrence has a direct connection to the story of the Holy Grail. In 258, when Valerian's persecutions grew worse, Lawrence was the Spanish deacon in Rome, where he received the chalice of the Last Supper from Pope Sixtus II along with the mission to keep it out of the soldiers' hands. Lawrence managed to have the priceless relic sent to his family house in Huesca shortly before he was burned at the stake. After this, the movements of the Grail become lost in the mists of history and legend.

As has been insistently aired in recent bestsellers, the Holy Grail is the emblematic symbol of esoteric Christianity that claims that Jesus' lineage continued through the alleged daughter he had with Mary Magdalene. According to this version of the story, based on the gnostic gospels, there existed not only a physical chalice but also a document, relic, or formula revealing this Great Secret and other millenary mysteries. Without a doubt, Philip II and his esoteric circle knew of this heterodoxy and perhaps even had contact with some of the sects inspired by the mysterious Priory of Sion, including the Order of the Temple. As is known, in the eleventh century the founding Templar knights lived at the spot in Jerusalem where the Temple of Solomon once stood, and there, in underground galleries and cellars, they are believed to have found valuable treasures and ancient Hebrew manuscripts, including the sacred rules used in the construction of the Temple. Considering that Philip intended his palace to be a reproduction of this Temple of Solomon, it is possible that he may have promised to dedicate the monastery to St. Lawrence in exchange for some Templar documents. Thus he was able to pay a surreptitious homage to the Grail without departing from orthodox Catholicism.

An Homage to the New Solomon

Following a strict astrological order and using the architectonic parameters of ancient mystical monuments, the building of El Escorial exhibits measurements, forms, and proportions that gather all the millenary wisdom of Hermetic architecture. According to the recognized expert René Taylor, the geometry of the structure's lines and spaces points to the use of kabbalistic methods, alchemical principles, Llull's mnemotechnics, and Pythagorean numerology, as well as other esoteric resources.

Perhaps the intention of Philip II and his advisers was not only to copy the Temple of Solomon but also to create a kind of culmination of all the biblical works constructed by divine mandate, such as Noah's ark and the Tabernacle. El Escorial would be a unique monument, perfect and timeless, the magical center of the universe, the *axis mundi* so dear to religious and pagan occultism. Moreover, the creator of this great work, Philip II, would thus be recognized as the new Solomon, king of the world and leader of Christianity.

In order that no doubts might remain as to the biblical inspiration of El Escorial, the monarch had placed there six great statues representing the Hebrew kings of the Hebrew scriptures: Jehoshaphat, Manasseh, Josiah, Hezekiah, David, and Solomon. (See color plate 26.) All these kings of Israel had some connection to the placement, construction, or restoration of a great temple in Jerusalem, and the last of them devised and completed the last and greatest Temple there. The statues, placed in the open space known as the Patio of the Kings, were made by the sculptor Juan Bautista Monegro. It so happens that he, like Juan Bautista de Toledo, was another participant in the construction who bore the name of the enigmatic Essene prophet John the Baptist, Jesus' cousin and teacher who was highly revered by gnostics.

El Escorial was formally finished on October 13, 1584, and its appearance was at once imposing and austere: The great rectangular perimeter with the church dome rising out of its center was flanked by the monastery, palace, library, cloisters, and other annexes. The vast and sturdy lateral walls have long lines of stern, square windows, identical and without adornment and, like the Doric columns, making no concession to decorative caprice. Yet the monastic restraint of the facade and exterior walls is counteracted by the magnificence and richness of the interior. The entire complex has four thousand rooms, counting all the salons, chambers, living quarters, refectories, chapels, and so forth; eighty-six staircases; twelve hundred doors, and 2,673 windows. It is all luxuriously fashioned and decorated, with the addition of 540 frescoes and sixteen hundred paintings of incalculable value. The architectural ensemble is augmented on the outside by fifteen cloisters, seventy-three statues, eighty-eight fountains, and eleven cisterns. In summary, it forms a strange alliance between humility and grandeur, a worthy dwelling and future resting place for a magnificent and prudent king at the peak of his Solomonic splendor.

The tomb of Philip II in the monastery of El Escorial shows Pompeo Leoni's sculpture, begun in 1592 and displayed in 1600: praying Philip II, Anna of Austria, Isabella of Valois, Maria of Portugal, and Prince Charles.

Symbols, Books, and Relics

Some scholars with mystical inclinations have pointed out various occult symbols and messages in the monumental structure of El Escorial—for example, the row of zodiacal signs that passes almost unnoticed on the floor of the main refectory. This strip, in fact, is an astrological calendar, perhaps done by Haco, in which the months of the year follow an astral order. This row of signs also serves as a solar meridian for adjusting timepieces such as sundials. The sun is also present in another enigmatic element: The golden stone in the spire at the top of the temple dome reflects intensely the sun's light at midday. It is the resplendent symbol of a solar cult. Why should this stone be placed precisely in this position, and why is it the only golden one among the others forming the pyramidal spire?

Arias Montano, appointed by Philip II as the head librarian of El Escorial, decided to house books in two different collections: a visible library, with the thousands of religious and mundane books possessed by the crown, and a hidden library containing treasured mystical and pagan volumes. The books were placed on the shelves with their spines facing inward, supposedly in order to air out the pages but in reality to prevent visitors from reading their revealing titles. There was also an apothecary or pharmacy—now no longer in the structure—in which were kept, according to legend, mysterious elixirs and magical philters, which were prepared by learned alchemists to relieve the king's many maladies.

A meticulous clerk counted and registered the 7,422 relics distributed in reliquaries, niches, and cases throughout El Escorial. The cataloging did not include the great space within the vault of the choir, where some authors claim are hidden the original plans for the true Temple of Solomon. (See color plate 27.)

ANDREA PALLADIO
VILLA CORNARO
(1553)

The most perfect of Palladio's famous Venetian villas, Villa Cornaro, reflects the mathematical mysteries and secret techniques of ancient architecture, achieving a magical harmonic equilibrium. (See color plate 30.)

The Architect as a Magical Harmonist

In the mid–sixteenth century, near the end of the Italian Renaissance, a structural phenomenon emerged that would affect the architecture of the centuries to follow, right up to the present time. In less than thirty years, in the countryside within a fifty-mile radius of Venice, a host of isolated and completely innovative buildings emerged, all designed by the same architect: the brilliant and mysterious Andrea Palladio. For the first time since the construction of the villas of the Roman patricians, this artist built outside of the city edifices that were neither castles nor fortresses but spacious country residences of immortal beauty that existed in magical harmony with nature and with the universe itself. (See color plates 28–29.)

As mysterious as he was brilliant, Andrea Palladio and his villas endure even today as some of the most important references in architecture.

So powerful is the serene mystery exuded by Palladio's eighteen villas still standing in this area of the Veneto that many authors have searched for the reasoning behind them in a wide range of esoteric knowledge, from the geometry and numerology of Pythagoras and his music of the spheres to the Hermetic rules used by Vitruvius. Also of note is these buildings' perfect correspondence to Bach's fugues. According to the Austrian orchestral conductor Nikolaus Harnoncourt, Palladio's buildings are the most successful expression anywhere of architecture as "petrified music."

Residential Temples

Palladio designed his famous villas on commission for great families who had grown rich from the rise of Venetian maritime commerce. Navigator-merchants took long and tiring voyages, and upon returning they wanted to relax away from the bustling city and its courtly festivals—but not too far away, to avoid the appearance that they were neglecting their flourishing businesses. The architect saw in these rich an opportunity to apply his innovative ideas and his Hermetic studies, and in 1540 he built his first villa for the Godi family. It included three stories of open galleries. From then on, he had no shortage of commissions from other rich Venetian magnates, such as the Pisani, Caldogno, and Saraceno families.

In 1551, Palladio built the Villa Barbaro (see color plates 28–29), whose frontal design is typical of Palladian villas: The central facade resembled a Greek temple, with two stories and four columns topped by an elegant triangular pediment. This was the first time anyone had ever been audacious enough to erect a classical temple as the entrance to a private residence. The idea was imitated on many buildings in subsequent centuries, especially plantation homes in the southern United States. On each side of this central portico there were two symmetrical wings, known as *barchessas,* each with four round arches. These were used as stables and storerooms for grains and farm tools. The long facade was completed on each side by a dovecote capped with a cupola.

Thus the villa was at the same time a country house and a site for the family farm—a concept repeated later in Andalusian farmhouses and *casas pairales* (family houses) in Catalonia.

The Mystery of Villa Cornaro

When Masonic ideas were spreading throughout Europe during the second half of the eighteenth century, a group of English initiates chose the Villa Cornaro, designed by Palladio, as the place for the meetings and rituals of the first Italian lodge. Their reason for this choice is not known, but there are some who believe that the Masons knew this villa was something more than a pleasant country house and that it had been built by an architect who began as a stone worker (or mason).

This villa, commissioned by the aristocratic Cornaro family—said to be the wealthiest in Venice—is considered as the unparalleled culmination of the architect's perfect and enigmatic art. Built between 1552 and 1553, it constitutes the sum total of the eternal principles and occult symbols of architecture, which Palladio acquired from his reading of Vitruvius, the neo-Pythagorean Gianbattista Alberti, and the romanticist Sebastiano Serlio. Everything in the villa is balanced, harmonic, and somehow magical; viewing it instills in those who behold it a feeling of perfection that grows into elevated spiritual serenity upon entering its interior. Its measurements and proportions appear to follow a unique formula, repeated in precise variations, that is connected to the surroundings and—more inexplicably—to the physical and mental well-being of the occupants.

This sensation has not only been recorded in certain chronicles but has also been confirmed by the current owners of the villa in a book published in 2005. The American lawyer and businessman Carl I. Gable, an expert in Venetian Murano glassware, purchased Villa Cornaro in 1989, after his wife saw it advertised in the *New York Times*. Since then, the couple have spent every spring and autumn in their "second home," which is considered one of the ten greatest masterpieces in the entire history of architecture. Yet Carl Gable's interest in the Villa Cornaro was not entirely frivolous. He dedicated himself to studying the structural secrets of the building and its architect's mysterious wisdom, and he and his wife wrote about their gratifying experiences as inhabitants of a house that, in their own words, "transformed their lives."

In a recent interview on the subject of "his" villa, Carl I. Gable discussed the mystery hiding within its walls:

> This led me to the last, least understood, and most evanescent element of Palladio's work: the harmony and equilibrium of the interior . . . which appears to be present only in the 18 villas in the Veneto, and to have eluded Palladian imitators in other places and in later times. Palladio certainly intended to conceptualize and communicate his perceptions; but perhaps analyzing them is like analyzing Leonardo's technique in the *Mona Lisa* in order to repeat its effect in another painting.

Numerological Relationships

In his book *Architectural Principles in the Age of Humanism* (1949), the art historian Rudolf Wittkower states that the relationships between the measurements of Palladio's villas are based on harmonic proportions that occur in music, especially in Bach's fugues. Comparing architecture to music was certainly nothing new; Goethe had already described architecture as "silent music." In the early nineteenth century, the German philosopher Hegel wrote, "Music is architecture translated or transposed from space into time; for in music, besides the deepest feeling, there also reigns a rigorous mathematical intelligence."

If Palladio became famous among the great families of Venice for building residences that looked like temples, Bach sought a way to convert decorative and affected court and opera music into pieces worthy of playing in a temple. His fugues in the *Well-Tempered Clavier* (*well-tempered* meaning properly fine-tuned) have the same persistent equilibrium as Palladio's symmetrical style. Their beginnings and endings are rhythmically identical, as if one is asking a question that the other answers, thereby closing the fugue and creating a harmonic counterpoint of a progression of notes. The architect and the composer, both geniuses, constructed works based on the repetition and variation of a theme that returned to close upon itself. Perhaps Palladio, like Bach, knew that the secret key to the sublime resided in this harmonic equilibrium.

MUSIC

THE MYSTERY OF CELESTIAL HARMONY

Music is the art to which the greatest number of magical and transcendent qualities is attributed. All religions have incorporated music into their liturgies as a way of predisposing and elevating believers' spirits. For audiences at symphonic concerts or at performances of the innumerable varieties of popular music, or even for people who listen to recordings at home, music emanates an ancestral mystery that touches players and listeners alike, transporting both to higher and deeper planes of existence.

The Music of the Spheres

The relationship between music and esotericism goes back at least as far as the sixth century BCE. It was then that Pythagoras, the great hierophant of Hermetic science, discovered the laws of harmony and established a number of esoteric principles connected to music. According to him and his followers, music was the harmony of the stars in the universe and the human spirit itself. The master of Samos, who believed in the power of numbers, established the measurements of the intervals in the scale of musical notes and related them to the planets known at the time. According to Pythagoras, these celestial spheres had the same proportions to each other as did the musical notes, and each one emitted an astral sound corresponding to its place in the scale. Later, Plato declared that the essence of music was cosmic harmony rather than sounds. In the third century CE, Plotinus, a devotee of Pythagoras and defender of metaphysical cosmogony, considered music as a path to reaching the heavens.

The parallel between music and hidden harmony continued through many ages. In the early sixth century CE, the Greek philosopher Boethius established a new division. In his work *De musica,* he pointed out that there are three types of harmony: the cosmic, which is expressed in the equilibrium of the universe; the human, which corresponds to the equilibrium between soul and body; and the instrumental, which produces harmonic sounds and is what we today consider music. The first of these was the music of the spheres, which continued to dominate philosophy and esoteric theories until the end of the Middle Ages.

In 1596, the German astronomer Johannes Kepler published *Mysterium cosmographicum,* a work in which he combined Pythagoras's music of the spheres and the recent heliocentric theory of his colleague Copernicus. As is well known, Copernicus was one of the first to claim that the sun is the center of our planetary system around which all the planets orbit. With new astronomical data inherited from his master, Tycho Brahe, Kepler was able to confirm that the planets in the solar system move in established concentric orbits and that, in doing so, they produce sounds that reflect the musical scale.

Hermetic Inspiration

Kepler confirmed the ideas of Pythagoras and Plotinus, who had already spoken of a silent harmony of the universe whose chords resound like celestial music on Earth. This extrasensory phenomenon has kindled the inspiration of many great composers, who have given it voice with the aid of their exceptional creative genius. Perhaps they received in an unconscious form this suggestion from beyond our world. At least, it is certain that the majority of them had esoteric interests or became members of secret societies such as those of the Masons, the Rosicrucians, and the Theosophists.

In this section we will explore known cases of musical geniuses entering into a Hermetic dimension. This overview will touch upon the great classical and romantic composers as well as rock groups whose members allegedly made pacts with the devil.

CLASSICAL GENIUSES
AND ANCIENT MYSTERIES
MOZART AND *THE MAGIC FLUTE*

An awareness of the heightened sensibility of music in the search for occult truths and the revelation of ancestral mysteries had as a precursor the genius Mozart. (See color plate 31.)

During the second half of the eighteenth century, Masonry played an important role in European society to the point where it could be said that being a Mason was the height of fashion. In Paris, the influential figure of Count Cagliostro (a more complex and profound person than his detractors have admitted) undertook to renew and purify the lodges of France with his Egyptian Rite. In imperial Vienna, the lodges were treated with benevolence and their work in favor of progress was well recognized. Among their members were politicians, intellectuals, and erudite clerics who believed in the renewal of humanity by means of the moral values of ancestral wisdom. In the opposite camp were ecclesiastical authorities and courtly aristocrats who saw Masonry as the enemy of the Church and the imperial regime. This division was not very clear, however, considering that Emperor Francis I is believed to have secretly been a grand master of Masonry in Vienna at the same time that his wife, Maria Theresa, led the opposition to Masonic practices. In 1743, the empress ordered a lodge meeting raided, which forced her noble husband to escape by the skin of his teeth via an underground passage.

In 1767, an eleven-year-old child prodigy named Wolfgang Amadeus Mozart was convalescing from smallpox. Thanks to the excellent work of his doctor (a distinguished Mason), the illness had left no marks on his face. By way of thanks, the young Mozart set to music a Masonic hymn and gave the score to the physician. During the following year, he composed a small work entitled *Bastien und Bastienne,* which premiered in private in the gardens of the enigmatic physician Anton Mesmer, repudiated by mainstream medicine for his investigations into animal magnetism. His theory, known as *mesmerism,* is often erroneously equated with hypnotism. Later, the young Mozart fraternized with other persons connected to Masonry and to the Bavarian Illuminati sect, which had recently been founded in 1776 by Adam Weishaupt and was the latest novelty in the esoteric circles of Vienna. The ideas of this sect were not only Hermetic but also political, and one of its leaders was Baron Gottfried van Swieten, a patron of both Mozart and Beethoven whom the Illuminati implicated in an alleged conspiracy in 1791.

Mozart may have sympathized with the ideas of Gottfried van Swieten and his associates, but his Hermetic preference was inclined toward Masonry. As a result, in 1784, at the age of twenty, he joined the Benevolence Lodge in Vienna. He was not the first composer to combine his passion for music and an interest in esotericism. Claudio Monteverdi was an expert alchemist, the early operas of Jacobo Peri toy with mysterious messages, and in 1762, Christoph Willibald Gluck reflected his Masonic ideology in *Orfeo ed Euridice.* Soon after joining the lodge, Mozart composed pieces for Masonic rituals such as *Masonic*

Dr. Anton Mesmer, known for his eccentric theories on animal magnetism, was repudiated by mainstream medicine.

Funeral Music. According to some experts, his last three symphonies form a triptych dedicated to the passages of Masonic initiation. In any case, there is no doubt that his last and greatest Masonic homage was *The Magic Flute,* an opera he composed in 1791, the year of his death.

Messages in The Magic Flute

The era during which Mozart composed *The Magic Flute* was not a good time for Masonry. In 1781, Emperor Joseph II had prohibited the existence of any sect or order answering to an authority outside the Holy Roman Empire (the Austrian Masons belonged to the Grand Lodge of Scotland), and the Illuminati of Bavaria had been suppressed and persecuted. The Viennese lodges stayed on the defensive, protected by their organic secretiveness and the connections they maintained in the palace. A new decree in 1785 subjected to strict police control their meetings and the number of their participants. Shortly after this, the alleged role of Masonry in the outbreak of the French Revolution caused the Austrian lodges to be condemned.

In this climate of intimidation and persecution, Mozart and his comrade Emanuel Schikaneder, an actor and librettist who was a member of another lodge in Vienna, met to produce *The Magic Flute.* Their idea was to conceal emblematic messages of Masonic ideology beneath an innocent fable so that these messages would endure and be rediscovered in better times. The expulsion of the Masons from Vienna had already been threatened; Mozart's intent was to compose a work that could be performed in European capitals and, at the same time, would hide within it a message of Masonic reaffirmation for the initiates of other nations. As another Mason, Johann Wolfgang von Goethe, later said, *The Magic Flute* "has what is necessary for the common people to enjoy the spectacle, while at the same time the initiated can grasp its noble significance."

Of course, the opera contains no explicit references to Masonry, although there are plenty of significant traces of it in the music's heterogeneous composition. The plot revolves around Prince Tamino and

Schikaneder, actor and member of a Viennese lodge, played Papageno in the premiere of The Magic Flute.

his search for the mysterious Queen of the Night, of whom his father has spoken. At the beginning, Tamino appears dressed in Japanese attire, which gives an Asian touch to the work, perhaps to distract from its Masonic background. The prince is menaced by a serpent, which is killed by three veiled ladies sent by the Queen of the Night. The bird catcher Papageno then appears and takes credit for having saved the prince. The ladies punish him by locking shut his mouth so that he cannot gossip about what has happened. They then show Tamino a portrait of Princess Pamina, the queen's daughter, who has been kidnapped by the wicked Moor Monostatos. The prince prepares to go and save her, and, to aid him, the ladies give him a magic flute, to which

Papageno adds a chime of bells (a *strumento d'acciaio,* "instrument of steel," in the original libretto).

Guided by three boys, Tamino visits three temples: the Temple of Wisdom, the Temple of Reason, and the Temple of Nature. He then meets Sarastro (an obvious derivation from Zoroaster), who shows him the place where Pamina is imprisoned. When the prince and Papageno arrive, Monostatos detains them, but Papageno's magic bells force the Moor to free them. Sarastro then arrives with his retinue and chastises the Moor for his misdeeds. Upon seeing Tamino and Pamina together, Sarastro forces them to separate so that each may face alone the ordeals that await him and her. The prince, princess, and Papageno each overcome a series of challenges, and, as a prize, Papageno receives a mimetic companion called Papagena. Tamino and Pamina finally pass the Tests of Fire and Water, the last steps in the complete awakening of mind and spirit, thus vanquishing the evil powers represented by the Queen of the Night.

With a fairy-tale plot, exotic characters, and an exquisitely composed score, *The Magic Flute* combines all the ingredients necessary to enchant both the common people and the most exacting music lovers. At the same time, it contains unequivocal Masonic symbols and coded messages composed by Mozart and Schikaneder. Above all, the main theme of the work focuses on the process that leads the human being to overcome successive challenges along the way to achieving spiritual and moral plenitude. This process represents the path of the Mason constructing his own Work. Once Tamino has proved his personal attributes of bravery, humanity, and intuition, Sarastro sets for him ordeals that he must pass. Having overcome these, he is united with Pamina, who has also passed through the initiatory itinerary required by Masonry. Director Ingmar Bergman interpreted the plot in this manner, distributing several compasses—the Masonic symbol of the Great Architect of the Universe—throughout the scenery of his film version of *The Magic Flute.*

The serpent pursuing Tamino at the beginning of the opera is none other than the serpent in Genesis who incited Eve to taste the fruit of the Tree of Knowledge, the true consciousness of good and evil. Thus the Queen of the Night—that is, the Queen of Evil—sends the three veiled ladies to prevent the serpent from reaching the prince. The repetition of the numeral 3—in the ladies, the boys, and the temples—is a clear allusion to this number's numerological significance: It represents the equilibrium between creative and destructive force. Sarastro is the high priest, the hierophant, initiator, and revealer of the Hermetic Mysteries. He presides over the most solemn moments in the work, such as the initiation scene in front of the pyramid (which, along with its great esoteric significance, is another Masonic symbol) and the final scene of the union of the princess and prince, the true culmination of the purifying process.

Goethe and other writers have connected Sarastro's nobility and wisdom to the figure of Ignaz von Born, a recognized individual of the epoch who was an expert in the Masonic symbolism that Mozart admired. Because von Born was considered highly suspect by the Viennese authorities, Mozart equated him with the simple character of Papageno, whose tonal, meaningless songs distracted the public and dissimulated the occult intention of the opera.

Ignaz von Born was an expert in Masonry identified by some scholars as the figure on which Mozart based the character of Papageno.

Mozart in 1789, two years
before he succumbed to
rheumatic fever.

The premiere of *The Magic Flute* took place at the small Theater an der Wien on September 30, 1791. Wolfgang Amadeus Mozart directed the orchestra in the first two performances but had to abandon the podium as his health declined. Even on his deathbed the composer attempted unsuccessfully to finish his famous *Requiem,* but he died of rheumatic fever on December 5 of the same year.

CLASSICAL GENIUSES AND ANCIENT MYSTERIES: THE ENIGMATIC BEETHOVEN

Ludwig van Beethoven (see color plate 32), considered, along with Bach and Mozart, to be one of the three greatest geniuses in the history of music, lived and worked in an environment suffused with esotericism. His composition master in Bonn, Christian Neefe, was a known Mason and probably a member of the secret Illuminati. His influence over the young Ludwig lasted from 1781 to 1792, and during these years he instilled in his protégé the Enlightenment movement's ideals of liberty and fraternity as viewed through the prism of Masonic esotericism. Beethoven read idealist philosophers such as Schelling and Schlegel who were profoundly influenced by mythology; the final movement of his magnificent *Ninth Symphony* has Friedrich Schiller's poem "Ode to Joy" as its choral text. One verse of this poem reads: "Joy, thou glorious spark of heaven, Daughter of Elysium." Obvious is the allusion to the Elysian Fields, the paradisal place reserved for the noblest souls in Greek mythology.

Beethoven, born and raised Catholic, composed several religious works, such as the *Missa Solemnis* and the *Mass in C.* Nonetheless, his teacher Joseph Haydn considered him to be a complete atheist, while his friend and biographer Anton Schindler wrote that he was inclined toward deism. The deist believed in the existence of a creating God but did not accept religions, temples, or liturgies. In a way, this God is similar to the Great Architect in Masonic doctrine. Goethe, on the other hand, wrote that the great composer was strongly attracted to pantheism and that his principal deity was music itself. Beethoven seemed to confirm this, stating that "Goethe is alive, and he wants us all to live with him. That is why he can be set to music."

Whether he was a deist, pagan, pantheist, or perhaps all of these simultaneously, Beethoven declared in one of his manuscripts that "God is closer to me than to others of my art," as if he believed he was chosen to find divine elevation through and within music. This statement, more mystical than it is Catholic, bears witness to the composer's conflict-ridden relationship with his parents. According to several documentary sources, Beethoven never attended church, and it is said that he abhorred clerics. It is more likely that his closest approach to formal and organized worship occurred in his connection to Masonry, which was encouraged early on by his teacher Neefe. Yet there is no historical documentation for his Masonic adherence and the only tangible indication we have of it is the dedication of his piano sonata *Opus 28* to the known Masonic grand master Joseph von Sonnenfels.

When Beethoven lay on his deathbed in 1827, his friends decided to call a curate to give him Extreme Unction, even though the composer was opposed to this. Beethoven tolerated the priest's prayers and gesticulations, perhaps, for once, glad of his deafness. As soon as the priest left, Beethoven supposedly said to those present, with a wink, "Applaud, my friends. The comedy is over!"

Beethoven's piano sonata Opus 28 *was dedicated to the Masonic grand master Joseph von Sonnenfels.*

Ludwig van Beethoven died soon after, on March 26 of that year, leaving behind the mystery of his diffuse beliefs and the certainty of his genius expressed in a body of work as exceptional as it was innovative. Music history has declared him the turning point between Classicism and Romanticism, and, in search of a distant and occult truth, many of the great Romantic composers in the following decades passed on the torch he had lit.

THE MYSTIC LIBERATION OF SOUNDS
WAGNER, DEBUSSY, SATIE, SCRIABIN, AND CAGE

The exploration and renewal connected to occultism and metaphysics leads to a complete dissection of the forms of music as we search for its essence as a bridge to cosmic divinity.

Richard Wagner

The flourishing of Romanticism in the mid-nineteenth century involved a return to pagan myths and medieval legends, as well as an opposition to the positivist rationalism of the Enlightenment of the previous century. In its artistic expression, this phenomenon represented a reevaluation of esoteric doctrine and mystical wisdom, which became especially resonant in the works of great composers.

The fullest expression of Romantic regressionism was manifested almost solely by Richard Wagner, who resurrected Nordic sagas in order to produce an enormous elegy to the supposed superior virtues of the Aryan race. Wagner's great masterpiece was *The Ring of the Nibelung,* a lengthy, operatic tetralogy described by the composer as "total theater" in which he displays immense music as well as an excess of patriotism and personal megalomania. The German composer had no disciples or emulators, thus his bombastic conception of musical art died with him, though its racist content later served as inspiration for the theories and justifications of Nazism.

Before Wagner's talent left to humanity his controversial legacy, another key figure in the relationship between music and Romantic thought was the German Ernst Theodor Amadeus (E. T. A.) Hoffmann, who had changed his original third name to honor Mozart's genius. Born in 1776, Hoffmann was a writer, music critic, draftsman, and caricaturist, and in his free time he also practiced musical composition. Among his multifaceted works are the fantastical *Nutcracker,* which inspired Tchaikovsky to write his famous homonymous ballet, and the story *The Sandman,* on which is based another ballet, *Coppélia* by Léo Delibes. His esoteric tale *The Devil's Elixir* inspired a Jacques Offenbach opera entitled *The Tales of Hoffmann.*

In his role as critic and theorist, Hoffmann's influence was decisive in the profound changes through which Romantic music became more transcendent. A pioneer in the genre of fantasy with some macabre tendencies, he illuminated the darkness of the human soul and dismantled the false harmony of the bourgeois spirit. Hoffmann's analysis of the most profound aspects of the ideology of Romanticism—which stripped the movement of its frivolous surface—guided the work of many composers, both his contemporaries and those in later generations.

The Mystery of Monsieur Debussy

The *Prieuré Documents,* controversial texts kept at the Bibliothèque Nationale in Paris, list Claude Debussy as grand master of the Priory of Sion between 1885 and 1918, preceded in this role by Victor Hugo and succeeded by Jean Cocteau. Because the Priory is the most strictly Hermetic and secret of all sects—to the point where doubts remain as to whether it has ever truly existed—it is impossible to find confirma-

According to the controversial Prieuré Documents, *Claude Debussy was grand master of the Priory of Sion between 1885 and 1918.*

tion for this leadership, but various authoritative sources do reveal that the great French composer moved in esoteric circles and had a mystical view of music.

In his youth, Debussy was deeply influenced by Wagner's music, and at the age of twenty-five he paid a long visit to Bayreuth, the musical mausoleum of the great German master. There he made the decision to reject the influence of the Wagnerian style and seek new ways to express his interests. Upon returning to Paris in 1889, Debussy went through what his biographers call his bohemian phase, during which he frequented literary cafés and artistic gatherings. In these circles he formed relationships with iconoclastic intellectuals and musicians, such as the symbolist poet Stéphane Mallarmé and his colleague and fellow poet Paul Verlaine, as well as the mystical composer Erik Satie. With them, he joined the Critical Fraternity, a more or less secret society that sought new paths for French art to follow and in whose publications Debussy used the pseudonym Monsieur Croche (Mr. Quaver). In his articles he criticized traditional conventions in the style of Saint-Saëns, spoke out against the excessive Germanization of French music, and suggested searching for inspiration in Greek paganism and ancestral myths.

The Critical Fraternity and its circles were frequented by enigmatic and diverse individuals. Verlaine introduced Debussy to Victor Hugo, the composer's alleged predecessor in the role of grand master of the Priory of Sion. Debussy also knew the Belgian writer Maurice Maeterlinck, author of esoteric works such as *The Blue Bird* and *Pelleas and Melisande,* for which Debussy composed a highly successful opera with a double message. During the same period, the composer came into contact with Count Villiers de L'Isle-Adam, author of *Axël,* a story of Rosicrucian inspiration, which Debussy wanted to make into an opera, though the project never materialized. Numerous illustrious literary people with mysterious inclinations were members of the Critical Fraternity or at least attended its meetings: Oscar Wilde, André Gide, Marcel Proust, Stefan George, and many others, some of them connected with the Rosicrucian Order.

*Emma Calvé, a singer and occultist,
had a close relationship with Debussy.*

According to certain sources, Debussy also had a very close relationship with the opera singer and occultist Emma Calvé, the alleged lover of Bérenger Saunière, the abbot who discovered the Christological documents of Rennes-le-Château. Calvé allegedly introduced Debussy to Emile Hoffet, the priest of Saint-Sulpice who deciphered Saunière's scrolls; MacGregor Mathers, founder of the Hermetic Order of the Golden Dawn; and the Spanish-born French physician and occultist Gérard Encausse, who practiced thaumaturgy and hypnotism under the esoteric name Papus and who was also the founder of a kabbalistic branch of the versatile Rosicrucian Order.

It is not precisely known to what point Claude Debussy adhered to these people's theories or how much they influenced his work as a composer. It is highly probable that he participated in some Rosicrucian rituals, and he was undoubtedly interested in Christian esotericism and the discoveries at Rennes-le-Château. His first great masterpiece was *Prelude to the Afternoon of a Faun,* inspired by a poem written by Mallarmé and first performed in 1894. Conceived as the first part of a larger piece that was to include an *Interlude* and a *Paraphrase*— which Debussy never wrote—it caused a veritable scandal with its erratic sonority and lack of any definite theme. The composer wrote,

"I wanted to achieve a music that was truly free of the leitmotif or was structured around a continuous leitmotif that nothing interrupts and that never returns to itself." His greatest work, also with a mythological and pagan theme, was *Pelleas and Melisande,* based on Maeterlinck's poem, a lyrical drama which sought a musical expression for the mysteries suggested by the Belgian author.

Erik Satie, the Phonometrician

One night, while dining at the Auberge du Clou restaurant—which today still exists in Paris—Claude Debussy felt himself drawn to the pianist who was interpreting a number of unusual popular pieces in his own style. When Debussy invited him to his table, the young man introduced himself as Erik Satie, a phonometrician. Then to Debussy's fascination and astonishment, he explained that rather than making music, he made an environment of sounds. Satie added that music was contaminated by decorations and banalities and that his intent was to strip it of all these overlays in order to rediscover its minimal and transcendent expression—that is, to reveal the music of the spheres.

Satie grew to occupy a unique and eccentric place among the French composers of the *fin de siècle,* performing the minimalist stripping that he had described to Debussy. A virtuoso instrumentalist, he had worked as a pianist at Le Chat Noir cabaret before playing at the Auberge du Clou. In truth, however, he despised popular Parisian melodies (in fact, *all* melodies) and had already composed works of rigorous harmonic economy that were similar to Gregorian chant—pieces such as *Ogives, Sarabande,* and the three *Gymnopédies,* some of which were orchestrated by Debussy himself.

In 1890, Satie's interest in mystical esotericism led him to connect to Sar Péladan, a Rosicrucian grand master who had founded a dissident branch that was linked to Christian Hermeticism: the Order of the Temple and the Holy Grail. Satie joined this sect as its official musical composer for Péladan's Hermetic pieces. Later, he left this group to found his own lodge, the Metropolitan Church of Art of Jesus the

Conductor, of which he was the only member. During this epoch, he composed his *Mass for the Poor* (1895), a deliberately archaic and minimalist work that revolved inextricably around its theme and, according to some critics, appeared to reject any kind of creative impulse. Satie retired to Arcueil to lick his wounds, and there he composed a series of piano works with bizarre and humorous titles such as *Three Fragments in the Form of a Pear* (1903).

Around 1905, Erik Satie, on suggestion from his friend and patron Claude Debussy, enrolled in the Schola Cantorum to study counterpoint. His intent was to enrich his musical syntax, even though he was nearing forty years old, was already a fairly well-known composer, and abhorred the traditional philosophy of Saint-Saëns, which the school followed. His decision to return to academic sources, despite his opposition to academia, was a source of mockery for his detractors. Nevertheless, the Cubist ballet *Parade,* which he composed in collaboration with Jean Cocteau, allowed Satie to use his new technical perfection to open the way to what he called "musical objective." In 1918, Satie presented his most audacious work, the symphonic drama *Socrates,* which he wrote for chamber orchestra, soprano, and three mezzo-sopranos. In this work, the phonometrician composer attained

In Socrates, *Erik Satie attempted an approximation of the music of the spheres, a Hermetic tradition that originated from Pythagoreanism.*

an almost absolute level of musical and expressive minimalism through the repetition of ascetic recitatives accompanied by naked notes that sounded like echoes of the mysterious music of the spheres.

Scriabin's Theosophical Music

Western music has treated the Russian composer Alexander Scriabin with an indifference that borders on ostracism. Indeed, only in the last few decades has his work been timidly reconsidered. In his time, however, Scriabin was admired in several European capitals for his piano interpretations of his own extravagant and mystical works, especially his magnificent symphonies.

A visionary spirit with metaphysical interests, Alexander Scriabin (1872–1915) dedicated his life to composing pieces based on theosophical ideology that opened paths toward spiritual elevation. An exceptionally gifted piano player, in 1894 he began a brilliant international career as a performer and composer who was strongly influenced in both areas by Chopin's piano methods. His first compositions were mazurkas, preludes, and nocturnes in the style of his admired model, and this Chopinesque influence continued to shine through in Scriabin's explorations of more Hermetic musical areas.

Motivated by the success of these compositions in Germany and France, in 1903 the Russian musician left his wife and four children to begin a voyage around Europe, accompanied by his young student Tatiana Schloetzer. Their passionate peregrinations lasted for six years, during which time Scriabin developed a personal and original form of music that experimented with new harmonic ideas and different sonorities. The first completed expression of this quest was the *Divine Poem,* a work that received controversial acceptance from both critics and the public.

In 1905, Scriabin came in contact with some adepts in the theosophical teachings of Helena Blavatsky, a Russian metaphysician who had reintroduced occultism and Hermetic mysticism into Europe and the United States. The composer adopted the doctrine of his esoteric

*Scriabin used theosophy
as a conceptual basis for
his musical structures.*

compatriot, using theosophy as a conceptual foundation for his musical structures and seeking spiritual and philosophic elevation. In this period, he produced works with audacious harmonic transformations, such as *Poem of Ecstasy* (1908) and *Prometheus* (1910), which reflected his vision of music as a mystical bridge that leads to spiritual sublimation. In his last years, Scriabin was unable to find the inspiration or the courage to surpass these works, whose power had probably astounded the composer himself. When he died, however, he left behind a monumental unfinished project that aspired to unite all the arts in the composition of a great mystical work. This frustrated creation would have borne the appropriate title of *Mysterium*.

John Cage: Absent Music

In 1952, the prestigious American pianist David Tudor took a seat in front of the piano and remained in this position, without touching the keyboard, for exactly 4 minutes and 33 seconds. After this time, he arose, gave a parting bow to the flabbergasted audience, and left the stage amid scattered applause from a few staunch supporters.

This outlandish performance was the premiere of the piece *4'33"* by the eccentric composer John Cage (1912–92), which was denied the status of music by the majority of critics. Yet Cage had received a complete musical education from well-respected Pomona College in Claremont, California. He later studied under Henry Cowell in New York and in 1934 returned to Los Angeles to perfect his composition skills with the famous Arnold Schoenberg, inventor of dodecaphony, or twelve-note composition. In this period, Cage wrote his first compositions, following a strict atonal method of his own devising.

His adherence to Zen Buddhist beliefs gave him a mystical and austere sentiment, which was influential in his role as a creator. Inspired by studying Satie and Scriabin and following Edgar Varèse's experiments, Cage tried to strip his work of all academic musical connotations. He used prolonged silences between atonal and interrupted sounds, which were often placed randomly. In 1938 he formed an orchestra that consisted solely of percussion instruments, and in the following year he dedicated to this group his piece *First Construction (in Metal).* Soon after this, he began to use modified instruments, such as his famous "prepared piano," which had pieces of metal or wood inserted between its strings so that discordant and percussive sounds could be produced on its keyboard. For this strange instrument he composed works such as *Three Dances for Two Prepared Pianos* (1945) and *Sonatas and Interludes* (1948), an erratic succession of sounds and pauses that lasted more than an hour.

Because his compositions were not entirely tolerable to the concert-going public, Cage dedicated himself to composing stage music, especially for Merce Cunningham's contemporary dance company, which

Score for M *by John Cage.*

performed ballet with the same mystical austerity that Cage applied to music. He later abandoned composing in the strict sense, applying himself to using sounds from the environment or random combinations. Examples of these techniques are two pieces from 1951: *Music of Changes,* in which the pianist tosses coins in the air to determine which notes to play, and *Imaginary Landscape No. 4,* in which we hear twelve radio receivers playing at once or in alternation.

In 1987, the German musicologists Heinz Metzger and Rainer Riehn asked Cage to develop an opera which, according to their proposal, would be "the irreversible negation of the opera as such." The American composer produced five pieces that he called *Europeras,* which were created in complete obedience to the requests of his commissioners. The first two pieces premiered the same year in Frankfurt, the third and fourth were performed at the Almeida Festival in London in 1990, and the fifth was produced the following year at the North American New Music Festival in Buffalo, New York. The total duration of these works was 4 hours and 55 minutes, and Cage did not write a single note for any of them. Instead, his musical material consisted of a combination of operatic fragments from the eighteenth and nineteenth centuries, which the author called "ready-made music," or in French, *musique trouvée* (found music). In 1992, the five *Europeras* were performed in the garden of the Museum of Modern Art in New York City. John Cage died between the second and third performances, just short of his eightieth birthday.

Despite being famous as a chaotic and eccentric composer, John Cage attained great prestige writing books on his musical theories, giving lectures in the United States and Europe, and influencing younger composers decidedly. There can be little doubt that his work, which he called "nonintentional music," in fact had an occult and transcendent intention.

SATANIC ROCK

Inspired by occultists such as Aleister Crowley and filmmaker Kenneth Anger, satanic messages, which are either overt or concealed, have formed part of the ideology of modern rock groups since the movement's beginning.

Aleister Crowley was born in 1875 in Warwickshire, England. His parents, staunch believers of the Brethren Church, would not allow their son to associate with anyone but members of their church. Aleister was such a rebellious child that his mother called him "The Beast" (from the Book of Revelation). He later referred to himself by this title. His rebellion against the rigid restraints of traditional religion led him to study occultism and mysticism. As a young adult he was involved in the Hermetic Order of the Golden Dawn. Crowley later left the Order after being accused of publicly performing a secret ritual. Throughout his life he continued to explore the occult and wrote several books on the subject. His work was considered blasphemous and abominable and he was called "The Wickedest Man Alive" by the press for his dark activities in witchcraft and magic. Crowley founded the Abbey of Thelema, which was a commune of sorts, where the inhabitants devoted their lives to practices of free will, based on Crowley's motto: "Do what thou wilt shall be the whole of the law."

After a life of excessive decadence and drug use, Crowley died in 1947.

Kenneth Anger was a child actor turned filmmaker. During his teens he became fascinated with Aleister Crowley and the occult, and many of his movies reflect mystic and occult themes. In 1955 he made a documentary film of the ruins of Crowley's Abbey of Thelema.

During the 1960s, Anger associated with several rock musicians: Marianne Faithfull, Bobby Beausoleil, and the members of the Rolling Stones and Led Zeppelin. Many of these musicians appeared in his movies and wrote and performed the soundtracks. Two films produced during this time, *Lucifer Rising* and *Invocation of My Demon Brother,* were shrouded in mystery and controversy because of their dark themes and notorious association with the Manson family, of which Bobby Beausoleil was a member.

Kenneth Anger's interest in the occult brought him in contact with the founder of the Church of Satan. In the 1980s, Anger accepted initiation into the Ordo Templi Orientis, a secret society of the Thelemic Order, which bases its membership on a system of initiation that includes a series of ceremonies that use ritual drama to establish fraternal, spiritual, and philosophical teachings.

Hidden Satanic Messages

Rock and roll music emerged in the mid-twentieth century through musicians such as Bill Haley and Elvis Presley. On April 12, 1954, Bill Haley and the Comets recorded the precursory "Rock around the Clock." Three months later, the young Presley, at the age of nineteen, definitively established the new genre with his recording of "That's All Right." For the first time in North American music, there was no longer the obvious racial division; white musicians played pieces written by black musicians and vice versa. This fact, along with loud and stirring drumbeats, the sharp strumming of electric guitars, the howls of the singers (and the audience), and provocative dancing, infuriated ultra-conservative clergy and racist organizations. Even the term *rock and roll,* originally an African-American euphemism for copulation, was suggested by the provocative gyrations of Elvis "The Pelvis" Presley.

The immediate fundamentalist reaction was to denounce rock as destructive and immoral music that was inspired by the devil for the purpose of stealing innocent children's souls. Such arguments could not prevent the arousal of wild enthusiasm among young people, who elevated Elvis to the point of idolatry. In truth, the rock of the late 1950s was not so much diabolic as it was frenetic. But a few years later, as these young people reached adolescence, the impact of mass communication, the Vietnam War, the widespread use of hallucinogenic drugs,

Elvis aroused wild enthusiasm among young people, who elevated him to the point of idolatry.

and modern electronic technology created an environment that was ripe for the exchange of different cultural and religious beliefs, some of which appeared to have satanic undertones and secret messages.

A Demonic Web

The 1960s, known as the Swinging Sixties, changed the complexion of music forever. Popular songs were no longer just about teen romance and fast cars. Song lyrics became an important venue for expressing political, philosophical, and religious opinions. The Beatles arrived in America from England in 1964, and on their heels came the Rolling Stones, followed by other rock bands—all of whom rose to immense popularity and fame. Many of these groups were rumored to have satanic leanings, which were inspired by certain Luciferian gurus whose influence was growing in both England and the United States. The most notable of these gurus was Aleister Crowley. Although he had died in 1947, he served as Led Zeppelin's lyrical guide from the underworld and his face can be seen in the crowd surrounding the Beatles on the cover of *Sgt. Pepper's Lonely Hearts Club Band,* a psychedelic rock album released in 1967. In the same year, the Rolling Stones released *Their Satanic Majesties Request,* which was probably influenced by filmmaker Kenneth Anger, who was a member of the Process Church, a diabolical sect also adhered to by Charles Manson. As the leader of the cult referred to as "the family," Manson was responsible for ordering his followers to murder Sharon Tate, the wife of Roman Polanski, the Polish cinematographer who filmed *Rosemary's Baby* (1968)—which was released in some countries as *The Seed of the Devil,* in reference to the film's subject matter.

Manson's followers were linked to many members of the rock and roll elite. The cult members stayed at the home of Dennis Wilson, the drummer for the Beach Boys. One of the members of Manson's cult, Bobby Beausoleil, had a part in Kenneth Anger's film *Lucifer Rising.* Manson claimed that the Beatles' songs, especially those on the *White Album* spoke to him personally. He interpreted the Beatles' songs as a call to revolution and destruction.

Over the course of history, there have been countless examples of people consorting with the devil: Dr. Faustus, Daniel Webster, the witches of Salem, Massachusetts. In the 1930s, rumors circulated that legendary Delta Bluesman Robert Johnson had sold his soul to the devil "down at the crossroads," in exchange for becoming a master guitar player. Accomplished musicians have been accused of making a pact with Satan for musical virtuosity ever since.

It has been told that guitarist Jimmy Page, a great devotee of Crowley, convinced the other members of Led Zeppelin to make a pact with the devil in exchange for certain success. They attained this success with "Stairway to Heaven," an eerie rock song that has remained popular since its release in 1971.

Although the band has enjoyed extraordinary success, they have also experienced tragedy. In 1974, Led Zeppelin vocalist Robert Plant and his wife were seriously injured in an accident, and in 1980 the band's drummer, John Bonham, died. Both events have been viewed by some as part of the price they had to pay for their pact with the devil.

Many other modern musicians who have enjoyed fame and fortune have also been linked to making a pact with Satan. To better define this golden age of satanic rock, we will briefly review selected groups that stand out in its unfolding and propagation. Though this list is obviously incomplete, it represents the possibility of the essential presence of diabolical secret societies within the musical community, which continues to fascinate millions of people throughout the world.

The Beatles

Undoubtedly, the most decisive formation in the popular music of the twentieth century was the group that introduced unique ideas into rock and connected it to a great measure with their elegies to new hallucinogens such as LSD and later to the mysteries of Hinduism. The leader of the Beatles, John Lennon, has been considered a type of Antichrist by some fundamental Christian organizations. Lennon reportedly stated in 1966 that the group's success was due to his having sold his soul to the devil.

Soon afterward, when asked about the Beatles' immense popularity, he declared to the magazine *The Forerunner:* "We're more popular than Jesus now; I don't know which will go first—rock 'n' roll or Christianity." Ironically, Lennon was assassinated in front of his apartment in New York City on December 8, 1980. His killer, Mark Chapman, declared himself a fanatical admirer of the leader of the Beatles and said he had killed Lennon to share in his glory. There are some who say Chapman was the instrument of secret right-wing powers, while some believe the time had come for Lennon to fulfill his pact with Satan.

The mystical path that the Beatles explored can be traced in the album *Sgt. Pepper's Lonely Hearts Club Band.* On the cover of this album there is a portrait of Aleister Crowley, whose name can also be heard in "Yellow Submarine." In the famous *White Album* the tracks "Revolution Number One" and "Revolution Number Nine" allegedly introduce the group's first subliminal diabolical messages, which can

In September 1967, the Beatles embarked on the Magical Mystery Tour, traveling by bus all over England with the purpose of recording mysterious and paranormal phenomena.

be heard when the recordings are played backward (counterrevolution) and were discovered and denounced by Lutheran pastor Anthony Greenwald.

The Rolling Stones

Mick Jagger, the leader of this successful and long-lasting group, has suggested in various songs and on other occasions that he is Satan's highest priest in the world of rock and roll. According to some sources, Jagger was captivated by Wicca member Marianne Faithfull by way

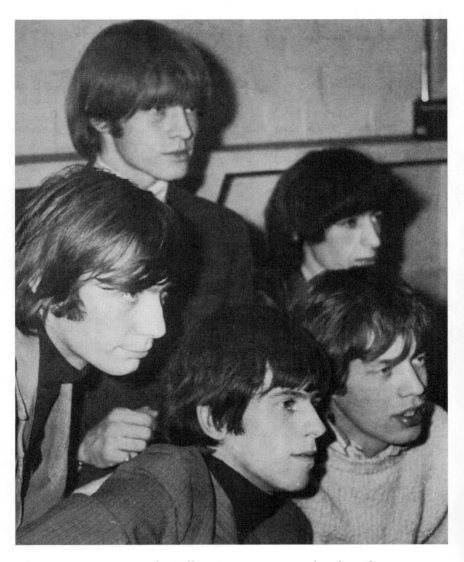

Their Satanic Majesties the Rolling Stones were introduced to Aleister Crowley's heir by Anita Pallenberg.

of demonic seducer and disciple Anita Pallenberg, whose occult arts enchanted Jagger and other bandmembers Brian Jones and Keith Richards. Pallenberg introduced the Rolling Stones to Kenneth Anger, who is considered the heir to Aleister Crowley's satanic throne.

Once introduced by Anger to the secrets of demonism, Mick Jagger was rumored to have been consecrated to Satan in a ceremony of the enigmatic Order of the Golden Dawn, a modern-day version of the mysterious Illuminati sect that was founded in 1776 by Adam Weishaupt. The Rolling Stones testified to their adherence to the infernal in their album *Their Satanic Majesties Request* and in such songs as "Sympathy for the Devil" and "Invocation of My Demon Brother," a song written by Jagger as part of the soundtrack for Kenneth Anger's film *Lucifer Rising* (later edited and renamed *Invocation of My Demon Brother*), in which Mick Jagger presents himself as the incarnation of Lucifer.

Beginning in 1968, Jagger began to diabolize his image, both in his choice of clothing and in his wild theatrical gesticulation. This reached a climax at the tumultuous Altamont Festival in California in 1969. While the leader of the Rolling Stones was shouting his invocations to Satan during the song "Under My Thumb," a young man named Meredith Hunter was suddenly killed in front of the stage, causing panic in the audience. The perpetrators of the crime were the members of the Hell's Angels who, ironically, were in charge of security for the event. Mick Jagger later stopped making Luciferian incantations and exchanged his satanic image for that of a quasi village idiot. Today, the Rolling Stones, although well into their sixties, continue to be active, even making exhausting tours—which some speculate is perhaps further evidence that Jagger did sell his soul to the devil.

Led Zeppelin

The figure of Aleister Crowley also appears to be closely linked to the demonism of the rock group Led Zeppelin. Jimmy Page, lead guitarist, was a devoted admirer of Crowley. In 1970 he purchased Boleskin House, the mysterious magician's Scottish mansion on the shore of

Loch Ness, known for the antediluvian monster reported to reside beneath its waters. It is said that at this location Crowley officiated at ceremonies involving black magic and human sacrifice. Without going that far, Page certainly performed there some lesser rituals from his role model's repertoire.

Led Zeppelin's great satanic emblem is the mysterious song "Stairway to Heaven." The lyrics were written by vocalist Robert Plant while Page played some chords he had written. "For some reason, I entered a state of trance," Plant related in an interview, "then all of a sudden my hand was writing out the words: *There's a lady who's sure all that glitters is gold, and she's buying a stairway to heaven.* I just sat there and I looked at the words and I almost leapt out of my seat." The

According to the members of Led Zeppelin, many of their songs emerged as if dictated by something they could not properly define.

members of Led Zeppelin claimed that many of their songs emerged through a kind of telepathic automatism, as if dictated by something they could not properly define. Many musicians, artists, and authors have described this same experience.

Besides its cryptic allusion to a "sign on the wall" and words that sometimes have two meanings, "Stairway to Heaven" has become famous for containing some of the most controversial subliminal satanic messages in the history of rock. When the recording is played backward, listeners can hear words that have been interpreted as:

> Oh here's to my sweet Satan.
> The one whose little path would make me sad,
>   whose power is Satan,
> He will give those with him 666.
> There was a little tool shed where he made us suffer,
>   sad Satan.

This does not make much sense from the demonic point of view, but 666 leads us back to Aleister Crowley, who proclaimed himself "The Beast 666."

This number, common in demonism and in the realm of satanic rock, is an allusion to St. John's Apocalypse (13:18): "Here is wisdom. Let him that hath understanding count the number of the beast: for it is the number of a man; and his number is six hundred threescore and six."

Black Sabbath

During the 1970s, heavy metal bands became more popular. Led by singer John "Ozzy" Osbourne, Black Sabbath's loud and eerie sound was developed during the band's rehearsals next to a movie theater that showed horror films. One of the members thought if people are paying money to be frightened, why not scare them with rock music? Black Sabbath's sound became music's answer to horror films—even their name, Black Sabbath, was taken from a Boris Karloff movie. Using special effects, bizarre theatrical sets, outlandish costumes, and extreme makeup, Black Sabbath created a visual image of sorcery and witchcraft. Song like "Nativity in Black" that criticize Christianity have also added to the impression of devil worship.

Ozzy Osbourne has declared that he always composes his songs "in a state of trance," perhaps aided by hallucinogens. "There is a supernatural power that uses me to write rock and roll," he once said. "I hope this power isn't a demon, but . . ." This ambiguity is in keeping with Osbourne's constant denial of his Satanism, though he performs songs with clear references to black magic and the diabolical. The name Black Sabbath is itself a reference to medieval witches' covens or nocturnal ceremonies during which they offered themselves to the devil.

Black Sabbath's emblematic album is 1971's *Paranoid* in which Ozzy summons from his throat an otherworldly voice that can be categorized as satanic. Osbourne's recurrent themes include the supernatural, nuclear annihilation, fear of dying, and unknown powers. The group later abandoned their Luciferian connotations in their album *Master of Reality*. Black Sabbath is credited with the invention of mood rock, death metal, post-punk, and other styles from the last few decades.

Kiss and AC/DC

Despite the fact that these groups are fairly well removed from the first wave of satanic rock bands, their references to gratuitous violence, unrestrained sex, and sadomasochism suggest a certain fondness for evil. Both groups conceal diabolical messages behind their apparently innocent names. Kiss can be understood in terms of its literal meaning, but it has been suggested that it is an acronym for Kings In Satan's Service. The technical definition of AC/DC is alternating and direct electrical current. Some believe that the secret meaning of AC/DC is Antichrist/Death to Christ.

Besides its symbolic acronym, the band Kiss has raised glam rock to its most infernal extremes, expressing its threat in the chorus to the song "God of Thunder":

Some of the fans of AC/DC believe that the letters do not refer to electrical currents but instead mean Antichrist/Death to Christ.

> *God of thunder and rock and roll*
> *The spell you're under*
> *Will slowly rob you of your virgin soul.*

It is understood that this violating god is none other than Lucifer himself. As for AC/DC, the titles of several of their songs contain the word *hell*—"Highway to Hell" (which parodies Led Zeppelin's "Stairway to Heaven") and "Hell's Bells" suggest an interest in the dark underworld.

The satanic rock of the sixties and seventies in America began to lose its strength in the 1980s as young people's tastes moved toward more mundane musical forms, such as pop rock and its more or less rebellious and predictable variations.

Spanish Rock

As suggested by the names of some of its most conspicuous bands, rock in Spain has been more sinister than strictly satanic. Though the devil's footprints appear visible in certain areas, the main current of Spanish rock follows the trail of *post-punk* (the direct antecedent of what is now known as Gothic rock), in some cases with countercultural or anarchist references. The pioneers on the Madrid scene have been Parálasis Permanente and Gabinete Caligari. After these bands appeared, some heavy metal groups flirted with the devil in their lyrics—possibly more in imitation of Anglophone groups than out of true conviction—and the following wave of punk music took positions that were openly anticlerical and anti-Christian.

The height of Satanism in Spain occurred around 1995 and was centered around Álex de la Iglesia's film *El día de la Bestia* (The Day of the Beast). The protagonist is a young fan of death-metal satanic rock who assists an enlightened priest in preventing the birth of the Antichrist in Madrid. To this end, the two consult an expert on demonism, who officiates in a ritual invoking the devil. Although the

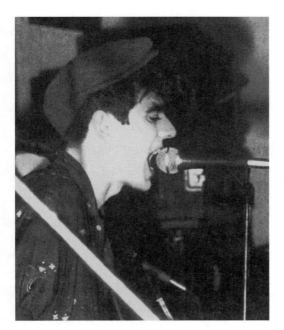

Gabinete Caligari at the beginning of its career. This band is one of the pioneer groups in the development of post-punk in Spain.

Álex de la Iglesia during the shooting of one of his films. The height of Satanism in Spain occurred around 1995 and was centered around his film El día de la Bestia *(The Day of the Beast).*

film itself is simply a madcap black comedy, its subject matter and its vibrant soundtrack—by the metal group Def Con Dos—awakened a passionate interest in the diabolical in young Spanish rock fans. This coincided with a general esoteric climate encouraged by the end of the millennium. Álex de la Iglesia defined his musical tastes: "What I like best is death metal; I enjoy the raucous voice of the demon, the total absence of melody, and the frantic rhythm that dissolves into a pure machine gun."

Although the success of Spanish satanic rock is not comparable, for example, to the international rise of the Norwegian group Turboneger, the self-proclaimed "Defenders of God" continue their search for diabolical messages, even sometimes where there are none. A recent example can be found in the lyrics to "Aserejé" by the Spanish group Las Ketchup, which was a summer hit in 2005 around the world. A Mexican cleric sent a letter to a prominent magazine denouncing the Satanism hidden behind the apparent banality of this song's lyrics. Beginning with the title, the seasoned exorcist translated the initial *a* as the English indefinite article and the *serejé* as the Spanish *ser hereje* (heretical being). The title thus becomes "A Heretical Being." The lyrics that follow include:

> *Mira lo que se avecina*
> *A la vuelta de la esquina:*
> *Viene Diego rumbeando.*
> *Con la luna en las pupilas*
> *Y su traje aguamarina parece de contrabando*
>
> Look who is advancing
> Around the corner:
> Diego is dancing the rumba.
> With the moon in his pupils
> And his aquamarine suit looks like contraband.

According to the accusing exegete, this is a clear allusion to the imminent end of the world (advancing around the corner) and to the nighttime demon who dances with the moon in his eyes and wears a blue suit (apparently his favorite color). With this smuggled suit (contraband) he enters into hell, where he no longer has a soul, and dances, possessed by a strange *ragatanga* rhythm.

This esoteric interpretation would be plausible were it not for the fact that Las Ketchup also recorded an English version of the song with a very loose translation in which "heretical being" does not make sense and Diego dances the mamba. The Brazilian girl band Rouge also recorded a successful Portuguese version, which deviates less from the original. In fact, the song plagiarizes (or pays homage to) "Rapper's Delight" by the American group Sugarhill Gang, the first hip-hop group to earn a gold record in 1979. "Aserejé" is not an invocation of the devil but is instead a made-up Spanish word used intentionally by the writer, Queco Ruiz, to translate the first line of "Rapper's Delight":

I said a hip hop a hippie the hippie
becomes
Aserejé ja de jé de de jebe

Despite this fact, revealed by a prestigious German news agency, "Aserejé" is still banned from many religious schools in Latin America and from Mango TV, the station owned by the Dominican merengue artist Juan Luis Guerra.

The true leadership of satanic rock in Spain appears to be held by a group named Dover. Formed in 1992, this group sings songs in English such as "Devil Came to Me," which was also the title of Dover's second album. In 1999, the group recorded "Late at Night" in Seattle, and in September 2001 they recorded "I Was Dead for 7 weeks in the City of Angels," which does not refer to Los Angeles, California. Dover's great international success was confirmed in 2000 when they received the MTV Europe Best Spanish Artist award, beating great stars such as Mónica Naranjo and Enrique Iglesias—perhaps thanks to their diabolical arts.

✠ ✠ ✠

As the text and illustrations here show, symbols of magic and esoteric ideology exist in all art, from contemporary rock music to the ancient architecture of the Egyptians. What is important, though, is what artists, and their art, are seeking to communicate to those who view or, in the case of music, listen to it.

The function of art has always been to hold up a mirror to us as humans, but it also shows what is possible for us to become. If we approach all painting, architecture, sculpture, and music and the Hermetic ideologies expressed within them with this in mind, we can become attuned to the messages they hold for us and then use what we learn to alter our lives.

BIBLIOGRAPHY

Argan, G. C. *Renacimiento y Barroco, I. De Giotto a Leonardo da Vinci*. Madrid: Akal, 1987.

Azara, P. *Imagen de lo Invisible*. Barcelona: Anagrama, 2005.

Babini, J. *Leonardo y los técnicos del Renacimiento*. Buenos Aires: Centro Editor de América Latina, 1969.

Bazin, G. *Histoire de l'histoire de l'art: de Vasari à nos jours*. Paris: Albin Michel, 1986.

Bendala, M. "Reflexiones sobre la Dama de Elche." *REIB* 1 (1994).

Benz, E. *Les sources mystiques de la philosophie romantique allemande*. Paris: Vrin, 1968.

Bing, G. *Fritz Saxl: 1890–1948: A Volume of Memorial Essays from His Friends in England*. New York: D. J. Gordon, 1957.

Burke, P. *The Italian Renaissance*. Princeton, N.J.: Princeton University Press, 1987.

Burucúa, J. E. *Historia, Arte, Cultura: De Aby Warburg a Carlo Ginzburg*. Mexico: Fondo de Cultura Económica, 2003.

Carter, S. *Misterios de la Antigüedad*. Barcelona: Robinbook, 2002.

Charpentier, L. *The Mysteries of Chartres Cathedral*. Translated by Ronald Fraser. London: Research into Lost Knowledge Organization, 1972.

Cirlot, J.-E. *Diccionario de símbolos*. Barcelona: Labor, 1995.

Combe, J. *Enciclopedia Universale dell'Arte*. Novara, Italy: Istituto Geografico de Agostini, 1980.

Cotterell, A. *The Ultimate Encyclopedia of Mythology*. London: Anness, 1999.

Dalí, S. *The Secret Life of Salvador Dalí*. New York: Dial Press, 1942.

———. *El mito trágico de "El Angelus" de Millet*. Barcelona: Tusquets, 2002.

Deimling, B. *Sandro Botticelli*. Köln, Germany: Taschen, 2001.

de Tolnay, C. *Corpus dei disegni di Michelangelo*. Novara, Italy: Istituto Geografico De Agostini, n.d.

Diderot, D. *Diderot on Art*. Translated by John Goodman. New Haven, Conn.: Yale University Press, 1995.

Donington, R. *Wagner's Ring and Its Symbols: The Music and the Myth*. London: Faber and Faber, 1984.

Ficino, M. *Sobre el amor: Comentarios al Banquete de Platón*. Mexico City: Universidad Nacional Autónoma de México, 1994.

Florensky, P. *La perspectiva invertida*. Madrid: Siruela, 2005.

Fraenger, W. *The Millennium of Hieronymus Bosch: Outlines of a New Interpretation*. New York: Hacker Art Books, 1976.

Fulcanelli. *Le mystère des cathédrales: Esoteric Interpretation of the Hermetic Symbols of the Great Work*. Albuquerque, N.M.: Brotherhood of Life, 1984.

Gable, S., and C. I. Gable. *Palladian Days: Finding a New Life in an Italian Country House*. New York: Knopf, 2005.

García Font, J. *La magia de la imagen*. Barcelona: Aurum, 1995.

Garin, E. *Dal Medioevo y Rinascimento*. Florence: G. C. Sansoni, 1950.

Godwin, J. "Escuchando las Armonías Secretas." In *Symbolos: Cuadernos de la Gnosis* 6 (1996).

González, F. *Hermetismo y masonería*. Buenos Aires: Kier, 2001.

———. *Las utopías renacentistas, esoterismo y símbolo*. Buenos Aires: Kier, 2004.

Hagen, R.-M., and R. Hagen. *What Great Paintings Say*. 2 vols. New York: Taschen, 1993.

Harris, L. *The Secret Heresy of Hieronymus Bosch*. Edinburgh: Floris Books, 1995.

James, H., and A. M. Shestack. *Hans Baldung Grien: Prints and Drawings*. Chicago: University of Chicago Press, 1981.

Kandinsky, W. *Concerning the Spiritual in Art*. New York: Wittenborn, Schultz, 1947.

Kleinbauer, W. E. *Modern Perspectives in Western Art History: An Anthology of 20th-Century Writings on the Visual Arts*. New York: Holt, Rinehart, and Winston, 1971.

———. *Research Guide to the History of Western Art*. Chicago: American Library Association, 1982.

Klibansky, R., E. Panofsky, and F. Saxl. *Saturn and Melancholy*. London: Nelson, 1964.

Laban, R. *Música rock y satanismo*. Barcelona: Obelisco, 1986.

Landon, H. C. *Mozart and the Masons: New Light on the Lodge Crowned Hope*. London: Thames and Hudson, 1982.

Livraga Rizzi, J. A. "Interpretación esotérica de *La primavera*." *Esfinge: Cuadernos de Cultura* 56 (2005): 24–27.

Maclagan, D. *Creation Myths: Man's Introduction to the World*. London: Thames and Hudson, 1977.

Mayr, F., and A. Ortiz-Osés. *La mitología occidental*. Barcelona: Anthropos, 1989.

Mellers, W. *Beethoven and the Voice of God*. New York: Oxford University Press, 1983.

Moynihan, M., and D. Soderlind. *Lords of Chaos: The Bloody Rise of the Satanic Metal Underground*. Los Angeles: Feral House, 2003.

Nácar Fuster, E., and A. Colunga. *Sagrada Biblia*. Madrid: Católica, 1964.

Olmos, R., and T. Tortosa. *La Dama de Elche: Lecturas desde la diversidad*. Madrid: Agepasa, 1997.

Pacioli, L. *La divina proporción*. Madrid: Akal, 1991.

Palladio, A. *The Four Books on Architecture*. Cambridge, Mass.: MIT Press, 2002.

Panofsky, E. *Classical Mythology in Mediaeval Art*. New York: Metropolitan Museum, 1983.

———. *Renaissance and Renascenses in Western Art*. London: Paladin, 1970.

———. *Studies in Iconology: Humanistic Themes in the Art of the Renaissance*. New York: Harper and Row, 1962.

Pingree, D. *Picatrix: The Latin Version of the Ghayat al-Hakim*. London: Warburg Institute, 1986.

Pita Andrade, J. M. *Goya*. Madrid: Sílex, 1977.

Regimbal, J.-P. *Le rock 'n' roll: viol de la conscience par les messages subliminaux*. Sherbrooke, Quebec: Éditions Saint-Raphaël, 1983.

Roob, A. *The Hermetic Museum: Alchemy and Mysticism*. New York: Taschen, 1997.

Salvini, R., and H. W. Grohm. *La obra pictórica completa de Holbein*. Barcelona: Noguer y Caralt, 1972.

Sánchez Canton, F. J. *Vida y obras de Goya*. Madrid: Peninsular, 1951.

Saslow, J. M. *The Poetry of Michelangelo: An Annotated Translation*. New Haven, Conn.: Yale University Press, 1991.

Secret, F. *Zôhar chez les kabbalistes chrétiens de la Renaissance*. Paris: Mouton, 1964.

Settis, S. *La fede negli astri: dall'antichitá al Rinascimento*. Turin: Boringhieri, 1985.

Taylor, R. *Arquitectura y magia*. Madrid: Siruela, 1992.

Teubner, B. G. *Saturn and Melancholy: Studies in the History of Natural Philosophy, Religion and Art*. London: Nelson, 1964.

Velmans, T. *El mundo bizantino*. Madrid: Alianza, 1996.

Viatte, A. *Les sources occultes du Romanticisme*. 2 vols. Paris: Honoré Champion, 1979.

Walker, D. P. *Spiritual and Demonic Magic from Ficino to Campanella*. University Park: Penn State University Press, 2000.

Warburg, A. *The Renewal of Pagan Antiquity: Contributions to the Cultural History of the European Renaissance*. Los Angeles: Getty Research Institute for the History of Art and the Humanities, 1999.

———. *El renacimiento del paganismo en Italia*. Madrid: Alianza, 2006.

Wind, E. *Pagan Mysteries in the Renaissance*. New York: W. W. Norton, 1969.

Wittkower, R. *British Art and the Mediterranean*. New York: Oxford University Press, 1948.

Zuffi, S. *Titian*. Translated by Sylvia Tombesi-Walton. New York: D. Kindersley, 1999.

INDEX

Page numbers in *italics* denote illustrations.